Praise for
Don't Let Me Go

"*Don't Let Me Go* drew me in with David's flowing prose and honest descriptions (especially about himself). David and Chera's story shows how extraordinary father-daughter relationships are, whether the surroundings are as mundane as the front yard or spectacular as a mountain peak. He demonstrates how every father-daughter journey can lead to summits of new understanding, awareness, and joy for dads and stepdads."

—JOE KELLY, author of *Dads and Daughters: How to Inspire, Understand, and Support Your Daughter* and *The Dads & Daughters Togetherness Guide: 54 Fun Activities to Help Build a Great Relationship*

"As a mother of three teenagers ages sixteen, seventeen, and eighteen, *Don't Let Me Go* came at just the right time in my life...in our lives. Many 'parenting' books preach to the mind; story always reaches to the heart. At this point in my journey as a mother, I need a gentle nudge, a hope-filled example, tender encouragement for this rewarding yet often treacherous climb. I am grateful for the privilege of discovering such trustworthy guides as David and Chera Pierce."

—LISA WHELCHEL, author of the bestseller *Creative Correction*, *Taking Care of the 'Me' in Mommy*, and *The Facts of Life and Other Lessons My Father Taught Me*

"David Pierce's accounts of the adventures he took with his daughter are as refreshing, funny, and exhilarating to read as the actual activities were challenging and strenuous. Each chapter is its own fast-paced expedition; each page a quick step of a fantastic journey. If I'm ever on a path up a mountain with either of my daughters—or heading anyplace else, for that matter—I hope I run into David Pierce, who can help show me the way."

—DEAN BATALI, television writer *(That '70s Show, Buffy the Vampire Slayer)*

"David Piece and his daughter climbed more than one mountain. The physical struggle of conquering a physical mountain pales in comparison to the mountains of faith, transparency, honesty, devotion, and forgiveness they each scaled. This gut-honest narrative of parental love and vulnerability evokes tears and laughs while providing valuable insights on how to be a positive influence on young people."

 —DR. DENNIS E. HENSLEY, author of *How to Stop Living*
  for the Applause

"The common 'push me, pull you' of parenting is joyously explored in David Pierce's new memoir of mountain climbing with his daughter. Pierce is the rare author and exemplary father who can combine warm humor with paternal anxiety. His story of reaching for the sky from the tallest peaks in America allows readers insight into what it means to hold tight to a teenage daughter's hand—and when to let go."

 —RANDY O'BRIEN, veteran book reviewer and journalist, and author
  of the critically acclaimed novel *Judge Fogg*

"I fell in love with the writing style of David Pierce more than thirty years ago when he wrote, *Do you wanna go steady?* on a note and passed it to me in the eleventh grade. So I married him. Our journey together has been filled with as many ups and downs as there are switchbacks on Mount Rainier. One thing we have never wavered on is our devotion to our children. They have always taught us more about ourselves than any wisdom we could instill in them. And I am so excited to have you read along and see for yourselves what God teaches all his children on the mountaintops and in the deepest valleys of our lives."

 —CHONDA PIERCE, comedienne, author, and recording artist

Don't Let Me Go

What My Daughter Taught
Me About the Journey
Every Parent Must Make

David W. Pierce

WATERBROOK
PRESS

DON'T LET ME GO
PUBLISHED BY WATERBROOK PRESS
12265 Oracle Boulevard, Suite 200
Colorado Springs, Colorado 80921

ISBN 978-0-30744-468-4
ISBN 978-0-30744-660-2 (electronic)

Published in the United States by WaterBrook Multnomah, an imprint of The Doubleday Publishing Group, a division of Random House Inc., New York.

WATERBROOK and its deer colophon are registered trademarks of Random House Inc.

Library of Congress Cataloging-in-Publication Data
Pierce, David W.
    Don't let me go : what my daughter taught me about the journey every parent must make / by David W. Pierce. — 1st ed.
        p. cm.
    ISBN 978-0-30744-468-4
    1. Fathers and daughters—Religious aspects—Christianity. 2. Parent and child—Religious aspects—Christianity. 3. Fathers—Religious life. 4. Teenage girls—Religious life. I. Title.
    BV4529.17.P54 2009
    248.8'421—dc22

                                        2008039502

Printed in the United States of America
2009—First Edition

10 9 8 7 6 5 4 3 2 1

SPECIAL SALES
Most WaterBrook Multnomah books are available in special quantity discounts when purchased in bulk by corporations, organizations, and special-interest groups. Custom imprinting or excerpting can also be done to fit special needs. For information, please e-mail SpecialMarkets@WaterBrookMultnomah.com or call 1-800-603-7051.

For my wife, Chonda. Thank you for your hard work, our beautiful children, and your gift of believing in me. Take away any one of these blessings and I could not have done this. You are truly the love of my life.

Contents

The knowledge of God is a mountain
steep indeed, and difficult to climb.

—GREGORY OF NYSSA, *The Life of Moses*

When you reach the mountaintop,
you're only halfway.

—MOUNTAIN CLIMBER'S PROVERB

Ascending

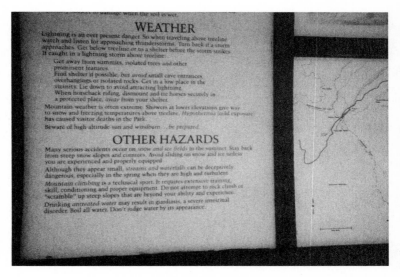

Mountain climbing is dangerous—
and that's not just me talking.

It was all Chera's idea. I just went along to keep an eye on her. After all, she was only fifteen and could get hurt out there, barely ninety pounds and so high up on a mountain like that. Since we had no special mountain climbing skills, we chose Pikes Peak in Colorado. We read there was a nice trail to hike and a souvenir shop at the top that served ice cream.

For some reason that sounded safer.

The sign at the base of the mountain where people parked their cars and where the taxi dropped my daughter and me off told us that it was about an eight-hour "brisk" hike to the summit. It took us three days there and back. During that time, we bruised some things and twisted other things. We ate stuff we shouldn't have and didn't eat other stuff because it was crunchy and wasn't supposed to be. Our fingers and faces swelled up so much that we hardly recognized each other. We came off that mountain beaten up, limping, and thirsty. We never expected the climb to be easy, but we had no idea how a mountain can wear you down. No idea. And that's how our adventure began.

Yes, *began.* Because for the next three years we would climb four more mountains. And in between those mountain peaks, we would run a couple of marathons—twenty-six-point-two miles. And we would see God, again and again and again.

We saw him on Blanca Peak, in a sunset that mottled the whole Colorado sky in a blazing orange. We saw him in a mountain lake, where trout rose and dimpled the surface. We saw him in the blowing mist of Mount Rainier, in the sanctuary of snow and ice that stretched out beneath a full moon from a point called Cathedral Gap. We saw him in a man who simply gave Chera his sunglasses to keep her from going blind and in a cook who made the best chicken noodle soup I've ever tasted in my life.

We also learned about hiking back down into the valleys, where blue lights of police cars glare and people die and hearts break and you can see no silver lining in the clouds, not this far down.

So this is a book about what happened on all those mountains and in all those valleys. Peaks and valleys that taught me about life. I climbed these mountains with my teenage daughter, learning about patience and fortitude and gimpy knees and the love of my daughter, who cares about such things. I learned about altitude and what it can do to your sinuses and that even on the grassy tundra of Mount Audubon that teenagers don't know the words to *The Sound of Music.* I learned about preparing and training, and the painful consequences you pay when you don't do those things.

And as Chera and I climbed and ran together, I couldn't help but reflect on my own climb up a different sort of mountain, one that took place long before she was born. I was about nine when I somehow lost God; just misplaced him, it seems. That was the same time that things around me began to go wrong, breaking in ways I was sure God could fix, if only I could have found him again. And I remembered how I figured he must have gone some place higher up where I couldn't reach—maybe to a mountaintop or something, since he was God.

So I set out to look for God, figuring if he was out there, I would find him. I would climb as high and for as long as it might take, having no idea how long and how grueling that journey would become.

What I found was a trail that wended through disappointment and loneliness. I made wrong turns and met a few people who tried to discourage me. But I was driven on by the memory of his being there—back before things broke—and encouraged by those who helped me climb higher. I learned many things about myself, some good, some not so good. But I did find God, in the end—right where I had left him.

And in the end, I believe these memories are worth writing about—what I've learned from disappointment and victory, from finding my footing on slippery scree and sliding down glaciers, navigating switchbacks, and trusting my ice ax.

This is a book about all these things that I learned about me. But, mostly, it's what I learned about my daughter, up there on the mountain. How I was able to hang on to her. And how I'm able to let go.

1

The Paperback Book

This is how we hiked up five mountains: like mules!

Our adventure starts one day not long after eight people die on Mount Everest. We weren't there, and we didn't know any of the people. We didn't even know there'd been trouble until my daughter read the book. And, truth be known, I couldn't even tell you where Mount Everest was.

Chera is fifteen and skinny with long, thin hair the color of weathered straw, with more energy than you would think possible from looking at her tiny frame. She walks into my office with a big paperback book tucked under one arm. Right away I notice there's no marker stuck in the pages, which means she's probably finished, and by the look on her face, I figure very recently finished—still floating in that happy-yet-sad state that always comes with finishing a good book. I tilt my head sideways to read the title: *Into Thin Air*. I've heard of that. People in airports carry it under their arms just like that.

"Everything okay?" I ask.

"Wow! What a story," she says, waggling the book in the air.

I smile. Yes, yes, that's my daughter—the book lover.

Then her face takes on a more serious countenance as she asks, "Do you think maybe *we* could climb a mountain?" She clutches the book to her heart.

Now I remember. This is a story about a group of men who climbed Mount Everest, and something went wrong—people died. I want to tell her that's why we read books: so we don't have to do what we just read about; we live vicariously through the characters on the pages.

"You mean, climb Everest?" I say.

She shakes her head and I'm relieved. "Oh no. That's too big, too far away. But I read about Pikes Peak on the Internet. It's a famous mountain in Colorado. It's over fourteen thousand feet, but not like Everest. So we wouldn't need a passport—or oxygen. There's even a live camera shot of the mountain, twenty-four hours a day, on the Internet."

"Oh yes, I've seen Pikes Peak," I say, reconsidering the obvious dangers awaiting young people on the Internet.

"Really?" She seems encouraged by that, prodded by that.

"Let me get this straight." I lean forward in my chair, where I've been minding my own business. "In that book you just read about mountain climbing," I say, pointing to the one under her arm, "doesn't somebody *die?*"

"Eight people actually, but that was Everest. I'm talking about Pikes Peak. There's even a souvenir shop at the top…with ice cream."

"How's a souvenir shop going to keep us from dying?"

"Come on, Dad. I read that there's a trail you can hike all the way to the top, so we won't need ropes or ice axes or crampons or a Sherpa or anything like that."

I do a quick search of my memory, trying to recall if I'd ever heard of a CNN crew at Pikes Peak reporting about missing hikers, but I come up with nothing. And what in the world is a Sherpa?

I'm not an outdoor adventurist. That's what I'm thinking as I'm sitting there in my office chair minding my own business. I don't run. I don't lift weights. Sometimes, when I'm going out for an ice-cream cone and the car keys are upstairs, I'll sit at the bottom of the stairs and think long and hard about how badly I want that ice-cream cone before I climb the sixteen steps to the top. (I almost always go after the keys—that is, if it truly means getting an ice-cream cone.) I've camped out in the woods a few times, but I can't sleep without a pillow or a mattress or if the smallest pebble (or pea) is beneath me. I don't like walking in the morning dew because it soaks through my shoes and makes my toes wrinkle. And when I brush my teeth, I can't stand it if the water's too cold. Oh, and I hate dirty hands.

But she seems so much older and bigger standing there in the doorway. Big and grown-up. She looks a lot like her mother, and I wonder where my little girl has gone. We've stopped marking her height on the door casing, but that's because we moved a few years ago. The new owners have probably painted over all that by now. With every yard sale, more little-girl toys go away for as little as a dime apiece. Last week she had her first manicure. Time is taking her away bit by bit. Time is sneaky that way.

And there are boys. They call. They sit next to her in church and at school. When she has a party, she invites them. And there's always a boy's name scrawled on her notebook. Trey. Ronnie. Adam. Ryan. Sometimes I see where she's scratched through a name, blackened it out with some permanency, but before long a new one appears. She'll draw it out in great detail with block letters and shading and depth, probably missing out on valuable lessons in geometry and world history.

When she was younger we'd play *The Pierce Family Show,* using a big mirror in the living room as our television set. Chera was maybe four or five, so I could hold her on my hip and she could see herself. The show would start with some music: *badadadadadadadumdumda*. Chera would hang on to me as we'd burst onto the screen, waving and smiling.

Me: Hello, everyone. And welcome to *The Pierce Family Show*. I'm David.

Chera: And I'm Chera.

Me: And together we are—

Both: The Pierce family!

More waving and smiling.

Me: We have a great show for you today. Don't we, Chera?

Chera: That's right.

Me: Today we'll be talking with a man…a man who… [I think up something fast] lives at the top of a volcano! Isn't that right, Chera?

Chera: That's right.

After we'd introduced our guest, we'd take a commercial break, mainly so I could set Chera down and stretch my back. I'd coif her hair with my fingers and pretend to touch up her button nose. And then I'd hoist her back on my hip and we'd count down from five.

Me: So here we are at the top of the volcano!

Chera: So what's it like living at the top of a volcano? [Chera would do all the interviewing because she held the wooden-spoon microphone, and I would play the guest.]

Me: Oh, hot. Very hot.

Chera: What do you eat?

Me: Hot beans.

Chera: What do you drink?

Me: Hot chocolate.

And so on and so on. We'd go until the next commercial break. When we'd come back live after this second break, it'd be time to wrap up and put out a teaser for next week's show. And each week Chera would bring back the man who lives at the top of the volcano. We totally exhausted the poor man; we questioned him to death. Once we did an interview of a man who lives in a hot-air balloon, but Chera asked him if he'd ever seen the man who lives at the top of the volcano.

I stand there thinking about how to answer my grown-up daughter and realize how long it's been since we'd played that game.

The little man who lives between my ears (no relation to the man who lives at the top of the volcano) suddenly pipes in: *It's just one mountain, David. And there's a trail all the way to the top—and a souvenir shop! She's your only daughter, for crying out loud! Your firstborn. She'll be grown and out of the house one day. She'll be a missionary in Mauritania and will write home to say how much she wishes she had a bed and some food. She'll write cryptic notes because the bad guys will be reading all the incoming and outgoing mail, looking for infidels, and she'll use code to say how much she misses the hills of Tennessee and that she sure wishes she'd climbed that mountain we'd talked about all those years ago, back when she was an innocent child of fifteen. But now she has too much to do in Mauritania before she moves on to Timbuktu. And "the cat's in the cradle and the silver spoon..."*

The little man can be cruel sometimes.

She stands in the doorway, leaning in, her eyebrows raised in hopeful anticipation. I suddenly think I should mark her height on the door casing; I could forever keep this moment. Instead I do my best to be assertive: "I...er...well, I...ah...if there is some way to...ah...I guess we could always...you know... You're sure there's a trail?"

She nods, but her eyebrows stay put.

"If you really feel like this is something...you know...I mean, it must be a pretty good souvenir shop and all—"

"Are you saying *yes?*" Chera interrupts.

I blow out my response, like a hiss, almost in protest to what I'm consenting to. "Sure, why not. It'll be fun." *Oh boy. Did I really say fun?*

Chera squeals and runs down the hallway. "I'll make a list of everything we need," she calls back over her shoulder.

She runs like she always runs, hands tight to her chest and elbows flying out to the side, feet shuffling along the floor in small steps, barely coming off the rug. She used to run like that from my truck to her kindergarten class.

Like I said, I'm not an outdoor adventurist. The closest I've ever come to thinking about climbing a mountain before is thinking that I would *never* climb one. But I'm a dad who's going to walk his daughter down the aisle one day, and maybe walking her to the top of a mountain will help me with that.

But then I start to wonder again. *What sort of things will we pack? Is something like this very dangerous? And does that souvenir shop really have ice cream?*

We'll climb on Labor Day, which makes sense to me. September 6, 1999. That means we've got two months to get ready.

I have a good friend in Colorado Springs, and I'm going to call him so I can ask him a few questions—like, where do we start? And, is it legal to just take off up a mountain in America? But first, Chera wants to take me shopping because I don't have a thing to wear. She has a backpack and a sleeping bag and lots of "survival" equipment like waterproof matches and a whistle to call for help. I have nothing. So she takes me straight to the hiking section in the JumboSports store and pulls one backpack after another from the display so we can check the linings and the pockets and the zippers.

"We're looking for one with an internal frame," she says, "and not one with big metal bars on the outside. The internal's a lot better."

"Says who?" I want to know.

"Says Larry and Lori." Larry and Lori run the adventure camp called

New Frontiers where Chera has been a junior counselor for the last two summers. I know them pretty well. We go to church together. They're about my age, and from what I've heard, they've climbed everything (with and without ropes), biked everywhere (always with bikes), and hiked in every sort of element—rain, snow, sunshine. So if Larry and Lori say something about the great outdoors, it's probably true.

"Okay. An internal frame it is," I say. "What color?"

"What color do you like?"

I think before I answer, "I'd like a blue one like yours. That way we look like a backpacking expedition—you know, a team."

Chera seems to like that idea too, so she picks out a nice blue one—big. "It needs to be a lot bigger than mine," she says, "since you're a bigger person." Again, that makes sense. We stuff the big blue backpack into the shopping cart, and it takes up nearly the entire thing, but there's still room for the smaller stuff, like cookware and an emergency candle and some Band-Aids and some freeze-dried chicken teriyaki. "This doesn't sound too bad," I tell her, as I read the label on the gourmet freeze-dried dinner. "We'll probably eat better than we do at home!"

We pick out a sleeping bag, and I grab a couple of those self-inflating pads to lie on, for both of us. "I can't sleep on the hard ground," I tell Chera. She just shrugs, and I can tell she doesn't understand. I start to say, "Wait until you're older," but decide not to. I figure I'll have opportunity enough for that line over the next few years.

I meant to call my friend from Colorado Springs sooner, but it's two days before we leave when I finally do. Chera's been training by running, mostly with her school track team. I've been doing some serious gardening—digging holes, moving dirt, pruning.

"Tim, how are you?" I say when he answers.

"Good."

"Hey, the reason I'm calling is to tell you that Chera and I are flying out there for the weekend to go to the top of Pikes Peak."

"Sounds good," Tim says, "There's a train that goes all the way to the top. Or you could drive up in your car."

"But there's a hiking trail all the way to the top too, right?" I have my fingers crossed.

"The Barr Trail, yes." *Great! That's the one.* "You can hike that…or take the train or just drive up in the car, like I said," he continues. I get the feeling he thinks the car or train would be the best thing for *us* (the inexperienced) to do.

"Well, we're just going to hike," I say.

"Hmm. Not a good idea."

Oh, of course, I think. *It's Labor Day weekend. The crowds will be awful. I should have known.* "Why's that?" I ask anyway.

Tim is pretty blunt today, which I can appreciate, since this is a long-distance call at peak-pricing time. "Mainly because you'll be traveling from about seven hundred feet of elevation to sixty-five hundred and then hiking up to over fourteen thousand."

"So?"

"So you're not going to have time to acclimate. You'll probably get altitude sickness—headaches, nausea, dizziness, maybe even edema."*

"Edema? What's that?"

"That's when your lungs don't get enough oxygen and they fill up with fluid and you can literally drown on the mountain."

"Drown?"

"Drown." *(Blunt.)*

---

* The exact term is *high altitude pulmonary edema.*

I think about this for a moment. Chera is down the hallway stuffing my new sleeping bag into the big zippered pouch at the bottom of my new blue backpack (internal frame). "But, Tim, we've already got the plane tickets." This sounds to me like an odd response to someone who has just told me that I—*we,* my daughter and I—could drown.

"I'm just telling you what I know," he says.

"Well, thanks," I respond. "And if you're not having too much fun grilling burgers this weekend, turn on the news and see if they have to send in a helicopter for us."

He knows I'm joking. "Be careful."

I don't tell Chera about my phone conversation with Tim because I don't want her to worry. And I certainly don't tell her mother. Instead, I rehearse the basic CPR routine in my head (five compressions, one breath, or is that ten compressions and then two breaths?*) and decide that if either of us looks the least bit woozy, changes color, or spits up *anything,* then we'll come straight back off that mountain. *But will that be too late?* Maybe we should cancel. This isn't sounding so safe anymore.

But I see Chera and she's dragging my backpack down the hallway, grinning. "Well, most of it's all in there," she announces between deep breaths and points to my fat backpack. "Do you have any aspirin?" she asks.

"Why?"

"Larry and Lori say that if we start taking aspirin now, we may not have bad headaches on the mountain. Keeps our blood thin too, so there's less chance of edema."

"You know about edema?"

She balances the backpack on its end and stands with her hands on her hips, her arms akimbo. "I know it can kill you," she says, quoting Larry and Lori.

---

* The current recommended ratio is thirty chest compressions to two breaths.

I glance down the hallway and then back at Chera. "Listen," I say, whispering, "maybe we should just keep that to ourselves."

She shrugs like it's no big deal and then goes back for more stuff, like aspirin.

People climb mountains all the time, don't they? We'll be safe. After all, it'll be Labor Day weekend and there'll be lots of people out there. People who can help with the stretcher.

Chera and I wrestle our backpacks off the conveyor belt at the Colorado Springs Airport. It's 11 a.m. the Saturday before Labor Day. We weighed them at the airport in Nashville. Mine is thirty-eight pounds, but I've got a lot of good stuff in there—valuable stuff, I think. There's a pocketknife that'll do about a hundred different things, like open wine bottles and punch leather and magnify stuff. I've also packed a collapsible shovel, a shiny bar made of magnesium that I can start fires with if I shave off tiny slivers and then set a spark to them, a two-person tent, some water bottles, assorted pieces of cookware, a Bible, a flashlight, a cookstove, some extra clothes, a pillow you could crush to the size of a bar of soap, a bar of soap the size of a pillow, and a blanket that looks like a small square of tinfoil. Chera's pack weighs twenty-eight pounds, which includes the chicken teriyaki.

We're both hungry. So we hoist the packs onto our backs and make our way to the taxi lane with our best lean-forward-so-this-heavy-thing-doesn't-pull-us-down-to-our-rear-ends strides. Chera's wearing a pair of blue sweatpants, the swishy kind, and a lighter blue T-shirt. Her hair lightly brushes the top of her shoulders as she walks, and she's tied a green bandanna around her forehead. We exchange embarrassed grins as we walk through the busy airport. We've never done anything even close to this before.

Already we've had an adventure. I'm pulling and tugging on a dozen different straps of the backpack, just hoping I'm wearing this thing right. We could be off to broadcast a new episode of *The Pierce Family Show.*

Out on the curb the cabdriver guesses we're headed for Barr Trail, and we feel good because we've found someone who knows where we're going. I ask him if there's a sandwich shop between here and there, and he grins and tells us to hop in. In the semi-clean little sandwich shop, with handwritten menus taped to the walls, I order a roast beef with warm swiss cheese, and Chera gets her usual pepperoni sub with mayonnaise and jalapeños. We bag them up and take them with us because we know we have a long way to go.

"There it is, Chera," I say while pointing to Pikes Peak from the cab. I think it's Pikes Peak, anyway. It's been a while since I'd been to Colorado Springs, but I feel sure this is it, since it's twice as big as anything around. Plus, I remember that when I was here before, the mountain reminded me of my eighth-grade history teacher, Mr. Jones. He was the first bald person I'd ever known. From a distance the mountain looks as slick as an egg on top, but is decorated with a fringe of green that loops about the mountain, about midway down. Those are trees, but from a distance it looks like tufts of hair framing a bald head, like Mr. Jones. Yep, that's Pikes Peak all right.

Chera's Internet sources told us that a man named Fred Barr started a trail in 1914 and completed it in 1918. During those four years, he'd work in the coal mines in the winter and save his money to buy dynamite so in the summers he could blast away big boulders to make his trail. Chera found out that the trail is almost thirteen miles long and climbs over seven thousand feet in altitude. There's a camp at ten thousand feet, about seven miles up: Barr Camp (of course), where Fred and his wife lived while he worked on the trail, blowing up rocks. That's where we're headed for the first night. We want to set up camp there and then go for the summit after a good night's sleep and some hot ramen noodles. But the map she'd printed from the Internet doesn't show us exactly *where* the trail starts—or rather the *trailhead*, I learned it's called.

The cabbie drops us off at the train depot and says, "Here you go! The trailhead is right up there," and leaves with his fare and (I think) a generous tip. Only, I'm not sure what a trailhead's supposed to look like.

We'll ask someone. There are lots of people here buying tickets for a train ride to the top. I lead the way into the train depot, but I'm still not used to the backpack, so when I turn sideways to let someone pass, I whack a display rack filled with key chains and train whistles and train caps. Everything shakes and rattles, and a high-school kid working behind the counter grabs hold of the wire rack to steady it. "Sorry," I say. I can feel myself turning red. From the corner of my eye, I catch a glimpse of Chera as she backs out the door, away from all breakables. "I'll take a couple bottles of water," I say, hoping this makes up for the scare I gave the kid. "And do you have a map of the trail?" I ask.

"We have this," he says, sliding a single sheet of paper across the counter toward me. It's a hand drawing of the train route that passes along such neat places as Son-of-a-Gun Hill, Ghost Corner, Lion's Den, and Hell's Gate.

"You hiking or taking the train?" the high-school kid asks.

"Hiking," I say, patting one of the straps that holds the backpack that nearly wiped out his little souvenir shop.

"Here's Barr Trail," he says, tracing a finger along a squiggly line on the map.

The map isn't the greatest, but it's better than what we got off the Internet. "How much for the map?" I ask.

"Twenty-five cents."

It's a chore to dig my wallet out of my pocket. But I finally do, and I pay him for the water and our new map, then slowly back out of the shop, waving good-bye with my water bottles. Chera's waiting on me out front with the sandwiches. I can tell she's been laughing. We walk over to a quiet spot where we believe the trailhead to be (according to my new map) and eat like hungry dogs while hard, tanned, skinny people with backpacks walk by us—eating raisins and trail mix. We have trail mix too, but I'm waiting to pull it out later, for when we're actually on the trail. And even though we eat while sitting on the ground and use our shirtsleeves instead of napkins, somehow I don't think the guys climbing Everest had ever squatted at their trailhead to eat a roast beef and cheese—but then again, as I think about the tragedy of it all, I wonder if maybe they should have.

When we finish our sandwiches, we stare at the map for some time, right side up, upside down, sideways. Finally, I ask someone passing by for directions. He points us to a footpath that leads from a gravel parking lot and up a grassy knoll.

We head that way. "Shouldn't there be a sign or something?" Chera asks me.

"Maybe they're trying to keep it like it looked in 1918," I tell her. *Yeah, that sounds right.* Chera leads the way. I can't believe we're in Colorado with heavy backpacks strapped on, map in hand, looking for a trailhead. This is getting sort of exciting!

Before Chera can climb too far up the trail, I pull my camera from an easy-to-get-to pouch and tell her to look back at me. She freezes and looks back and smiles. She even exaggerates the first step onto the trail, raising a leg and pausing with her foot hovering just above the packed earth that will eventually lead us to the summit. I snap her picture. Then, almost on all fours, she scrambles up a couple of steps and slips and comes sliding and scooting back down to me, knocking into me and my camera. I'm glad I'm there to catch her.

"It's pretty steep, Dad," she says, blushing and adjusting her pack.

"Maybe this is the worst part," I say hopefully. But my backpack suddenly feels so heavy. *I can't scramble up this hill! It's too steep!*

She shifts her load a bit and checks her straps. I snap a couple more pictures of this. Then she leans forward and tries again, no posing this time. Her boots slip a little at first, and pebbles avalanche down the path behind her and stop at my feet. Using her hands, she finally finds purchase in some large green tufts of grass on each side of the trail and pulls herself forward and up. Just before she reaches the top she remembers to turn and smile, and I snap another frame. She goes over the top and out of sight, comes back to peek over, then waves me up. "Come on!" she calls. Her bandanna is a darker green now because of the sweat.

Even from where I'm standing and looking up, I can tell Chera's breathing hard. I put away the camera and cinch down my belts and straps and, remembering Chera's struggle with those first two steps, get a running start. Bad idea. At almost seven thousand feet of altitude, and after a warm cheese and roast beef sandwich, running up a mountain trail isn't the smartest thing I've ever done. But I make it past the loose gravel and grab hold of the grass like I'd seen Chera do. I'm scrambling up the mountain.

I scrambled up the hill that felt like a mountain, just off the highway and at the edge of woods, because Dad had just driven by for the fifth time, and if he didn't find me soon, I was going to get caught by the dark. I was eleven, and Mom and Dad had been fighting again. Sometimes when they did this, when they filled the little hollow we lived in with so much noise that I felt sorry for the trees, that's when I'd run off into the woods and make them find me, just to give them something else to do besides yell at each other.

The first time I had a real sense of trouble at home came a couple of years earlier. We had moved from the city to the country, to a small house with three rooms and no indoor plumbing—that is, until Dad piped in fresh water from an icy cold spring on one side of the house and, when we were finished with it, piped it back out to the creek on the other side. This seemed like a brilliant piece of engineering to me.

On the night when things broke, when things began to go wrong, Dad and his brother were sitting in lounge chairs out by the spring. It was dark except for the light afforded by the moon and front porch light, and they were drinking beer. Just a couple of grown men sipping and chatting is what it looked like. But Dad never drank beer that I ever knew of. Back in the city the people who drank beer were bad people, people who stayed in trouble, smelled bad, and wore shabby clothes. That Dad was drinking beer made my stomach hurt.

Not long after this night, the fights started. Usually this only happened when he was drinking beer. When he wasn't, life in the country was pleasant enough (even more so after we got the plumbing in). I was close to God then. I had found him at Sunday school back in the city. So I asked him to help out: *Please put a stop to all this, would you?* And I thought that settled that.

Instead things got worse. More drinking, more fighting. Maybe God just needed a little help getting started, I thought. When running away didn't help, I decided to pour out the beer. Dad would try to hide it from me—out in the woods or behind the smokehouse. Wherever he hid it, I always found it and emptied every bit. Then I'd put the cans back like I'd found them. I don't know why. Part of me wanted him to believe the cans had just leaked out. Perhaps he'd think God had intervened, and this would make him quit. But when he'd ask me if I had anything to do with it, I always said yes.

This was definitely a job for God. Only now I believed I'd lost him somehow. But my family was too important. I would find him, I promised myself. Moses had found him on a mountain. I'd seen the movie. I'd find him too. No matter how hard it would be. And when I did find him, I would make him help me. Make him help Mom and Dad. So I set out looking for God, having no real idea of where to start, or if I was even on the right trail. And this is how my first mountain climb—that knowledge of God—began.

When I get to the top, Chera congratulates me by grabbing hold of my backpack and giving it a little shake. This is something that I guess back-packers must do all the time, since you can't give a real pat on the back and a high-five could send you straight over the edge. I want so badly to do that Rocky dance, but I can't celebrate too much because I'm leaning over with my hands on my knees and taking in great gulps of thin air and working to keep my sandwich down, all while Chera is shaking my backpack and saying, "All right! Way to go, Dad!"

When I can, I ask Chera, "How far do you suppose we've come?"

She peeks over the small knoll again and studies for a moment before saying, "About eight feet." Good. Only 6,992 more to go.

"It was a good eight feet, though, right?" I say, proudly. Then, stepping to the edge and taking a peek for myself, I say, part in disdain for the elevation I had just conquered, part in hope for the future elevation I would tackle, part in dread, and part in prayer, "Maybe that's the toughest eight feet of the trail." I imagine there's even been songs written about this part of the trail, songs about people dying and freezing in the winter and running out of food and all that stuff, right here, right on this eight-foot part of the trail we've just whipped.

Once I'm able to straighten to at least a mountain climber's lean, we walk on through a small, level grassy field, beneath some electrical wires strung through these giant metal poles and brackets *(Is this safe?)* until we come to another parking lot, only this one is paved and busy with cars and with people coming and going. Across this stretch of asphalt is a huge wooden sign that reads Barr Trail Trailhead, and there are people taking turns standing by it and having their pictures made.

"Oh look, Dad," Chera exclaims, pointing to the sign. "*That's* where the trail starts!" I'm still breathing way too hard when she sings, "Come on! Get a picture of me by the sign."

It was all I could do to hike to the point where we would start our great adventure.

2

Our First Climb

We flex our muscles at the summit
of Pikes Peak.

In a straight line, it's only about a mile and a half from the trailhead to the summit of Pikes Peak. But since Barr Trail is nearly thirteen miles long, you can imagine the crooked path we have to take. There's a term for all that zigzagging—*switchbacks*—and I learn it here on the trail from a man who just got a new pair of sneakers and is giving them a try. "I just did seventeen switchbacks," he tells me and then lifts one foot to show me his spotless white sneakers. "Just about got 'em broken in."

I nod like I know exactly what he's talking about. "Those look comfortable," I say about his shoes. He just grins and walks off.

Chera and I stand side by side at the beginning. *The Pierce Family Show* theme music plays in my head. We take deep breaths, look up the trail, and then begin to climb. It's happening.

Switchback.

Switchback.

Switchback.

I try to count the first seventeen so I'll know where the man with the new tennis shoes turned around, but after a few I lose count. The trail is nice and smooth hard-packed earth, lined with big stones and cedar timbers on the low side—to keep you from falling down the mountain, I guess. And is it ever a hot day. The shade afforded by the towering pine trees feels good, especially after passing through a long stretch of bright white daylight. The air is dry as well, and soon into the climb my sinuses burn with the aroma of hot pine needles.

We've walked for nearly an hour, and I can still see the parking lot where we first started. I can still see faces—I can still see *freckles* on the faces of people in the parking lot where we first started! Are we *climbing* at all? I don't think so. We just keep zigzagging and going nowhere.

There are a lot people on the trail this afternoon; most of them pass us coming down as we're going up. And with every size and shape of person coming down, Chera and I draw strength and encouragement in knowing that if he or she can do it, so can we: a group of kids, five or six years old, stamp past us—we push on; two bikers, moving fast, slide and twist around corners—we dodge them and then push on; a rather large woman in a spandex exercise suit, listening to her Walkman, sort of galumphs past us—we dodge her too and push on. "If they can do it, we can do it!" becomes our anthem.

We're about a mile up the trail when we stop for the first time to rest. We know we're about a mile along because Encyclopedia Man tells us. That's the name we give to the big hairy man with no shirt, who wipes his face with a fluffy towel and shoots water into his mouth from a giant squeeze bottle. We're leaning against a cedar railing and looking out over Colorado Springs. "You've gone about a mile," he pants, without our even asking. He's about forty and traveling with a companion who looks to be a bit older, but who has his shirt on and is neither panting nor sweating. "You are now on the fastest-gaining elevation trail in America—in the world," Encyclopedia Man continues between swigs of water. "And your elevation right now is about"—he squints as if he's having trouble adding the numbers—"seventy-six hundred feet."

Then his companion, the one with the shirt, speaks for the first time, pointing to the hairy man: "He's probably the smartest man in the whole world about this trail."

Encyclopedia Man accepts his friend's compliment and the title bestowed upon him with an embarrassed shrug and a slight grin. He doesn't look at us but takes another big swig of water, and then together they move on, leaving us to catch our breath. We meet up with them again at seventy-eight hundred feet and once more at seventy-nine fifty—so he says—before we hear him explain to his friend that they're turning back. His companion seems disappointed, but not nearly as much as we are. Now, without our walk-along altimeter to encourage us, we'll be climbing blind.

My friend Tim, the one who told me we could drown on the mountain, also told me that the first two miles up the trail are the worst. After that, it's not too bad, he'd said. So when we reach the two-mile marker, Chera and I want to celebrate. We lie out on the ground (because that's the best way for us to take our backpacks off now) and roll out of them and dig around in one of the compartments for some peanut butter crackers. We sit on a giant, smooth rock and take in the view of the top of some tall pine trees. "I can't believe we're here," I say.

Chera washes down her crackers with a drink of water and, looking out across a valley spotted with tiny cars and buildings, asks, "If I really like a guy, how can I let him know?"

Well, I didn't see that coming. But I'm sure she's given thought to this before. I imagine she's been waiting for just the right moment to ask me. I'm suddenly aware, even more than of the giant pine trees that surround us, of this "mountain" that she's scrambling up, only she's not scrambling to get away from me. Rather, she wants me to come along with her. She's asking me to. So I take a deep breath that has nothing to do with the altitude and ask, "What guy?"

She shakes her head. "Just any guy, in general. I mean, what if I like a guy, but I'm not sure he likes me?"

"And you're afraid that if he finds out you like him, but he doesn't like you, you'll be embarrassed?"

She nods.

"And you think *he* might like you if only he knew that *you* liked him?"

She nods again. Drinks some water.

"And although you don't want to be the first to say 'I like you,' you're afraid that he might be afraid to be the first to say 'I like you' because what if you don't like him and then he'll be embarrassed for saying 'I like you' because you really don't like him at all?"

She seems relieved that finally someone understands. I don't tell her that this scenario is as old and unchanging as the mountains. In fact, the same sort of stuff was going on when I was in high school: I met her mom in much the same fashion.

"Don't you have a friend who could give him a note or maybe ask him for you?" I ask. That's what we always did.

She makes a face as if she's tasted something bad. "We did that in the eighth grade."

She's in tenth grade now. "Okay. Well, how old is he?"

"He's a senior."

"Senior?" My voice is high.

She nods.

"First-year senior?" I ask. Then I drop my voice lower and add, "Or is this his second or third shot at it?"

"Daaaaaad!"

"So he's what—eighteen? Nineteen? Twenty?"

"He's nineteen."

"Nineteen!" I frighten away some pretty mountain birds from the trees close by. "Want *me* to talk to him?"

"Daaaaaad!"

"I don't know, Chera. You're fifteen. This guy's nineteen." *Hormones. Driver's license. Hormones. Car (or truck).* "There's a big difference…" *Hormones. Facial hair. Hormones. Hormones.*

"I don't think he likes me, anyway," she says sadly and takes a bite of cracker.

"Oh, he probably does."

"Really?" She perks up.

Why did I say that? Partly to make her feel good (and that worked), but mainly because I'm sure it's true. She's beautiful. Why wouldn't anyone like her? But before I can answer my *fifteen-year-old* daughter about how I really feel about her seeing a *nineteen-year-old* man with a mustache (probably has one), we hear screams coming from the trail, lots of screams.

They're coming from just below us. Chera and I stare at each other, mouths full of peanut butter and crackers. More screams. Shouting. Giggling. We stay put on the big rock and turn to watch a group of teenagers clamber up the trail and go past us. A man and his small daughter break away to say hello, and we find out this is just a small part of a Baptist youth group—about thirty-five people—from some church in Texas that came to Colorado to climb a mountain. Everyone is headed to Barr Camp for the night and then on to the summit tomorrow. We offer them some peanut butter and crackers.

I'm not saying Tim lied to us about the first two miles being the toughest (maybe he just forgot), but we don't make the first level spot until the four-mile marker. By now my lower back and hips are throbbing, and my legs are screaming. Chera is still leading, only she's taking baby steps now—and it's all I can do to keep up with her. It's about this time, when the pain is the worst yet and the baby steps are too big, that we run out of water. So not only could we drown (edema) on this mountain, but also we could die of thirst. How do you prepare for something like this?

Chera figured this would happen, though, and that's why she's brought along some iodine tablets. One orange tablet can turn a bottle of wild mountain water into funny-tasting, but safe, drinking water. We stop to rest, and when we get real still and don't breathe (just for a moment), we can hear water babbling through the thick green brambles and the aspen trees, whose white trunks are lined up like too many candles on a birthday cake.

"I hear water over there," she says as she points into the forest.

I take a deep breath. I know what we're going to have to do. "Then I guess we go after it," I say. Chera grins. She's liking how I'm catching on. Rolling up my sleeves and going for it. Surviving. We drop our packs and pull our water bottles out, and together we hike down a slope too steep to be hiking down with legs this sore. But we can hear the churning water, and we stumble toward it, pushing aside low branches. There it is! We kneel on the soft brown pine needles by the clear stream and splash our faces and bathe our arms. So cold. And then we fill our bottles and drop a small iodine tablet in each, just like Chera has learned to do at camp from Larry and Lori. I fill my bottle with clear, sparkling water and then watch it turn yellow orange as the little pill dissolves.

"So when's this okay to drink?" I ask, shaking the bottle like crazy, but the rust color doesn't go away.

Chera shrugs and says, "Just anytime, I guess. That's what we always do at camp."

I open the top and take a giant swig, and it tastes like medicine. I remember the scraped knees I'd had as a child and the medicine, the dark brown liquid, my mom would rub on to the wounds with the little pink plastic stick that came stuck to the lid. But I'm really thirsty, so I swallow it anyway.

"Good?" Chera asks.

"Well, it's cold," I say. "And most likely germ-free. Go ahead." And I hand her the bottle.

Now that we have water, we take some aspirin to keep from drowning. Then we pull ourselves back up the steep slope to where we've left our backpacks, hoist them up and on again, and continue to climb. After only a hundred yards or so of walking, we cross the same stream we'd just blazed a trail to a few yards back. Lots of people are here filling their water bottles, laughing, drinking, splashing their faces—kids, older people, people with dogs, people wearing spandex. We realize we'd filled our bottles downstream. Now I'm thankful for the medicine taste. We move on without stopping.

"They should put a sign up back there," I say. "Let people know they're getting close to water."

Chera nods and adds, "Makes you miss Encyclopedia Man, doesn't it?"

We've been climbing for nearly five hours now, and it's obvious that we're running out of daylight. In a grove of aspens, we spot a sign that looks like all the other mileage markers: steel with letters and numbers burned out by a torch. It tells us we're only one mile from Barr Camp. Chera and I try to give each other high-fives, but I almost fall over, so we settle for just saying, "All right!" and keep moving on. We stop one more time to rest on some big and perfectly flat rocks. There are lots of shadows now. The hot white spots have turned yellowish and are striped with long shadows that match tree trunks. We meet a couple of men who are on their way down when they stop at the same outcropping of rocks to rest.

"You headed to Barr Camp?" one of them asks me. He's tall and has a belly like me and wears a T-shirt with the word *Colorado* stitched across the chest.

"Yeah," is all I can say. I'm surprised at how much effort that takes.

"Well, you're getting close," the other one says, who is also tall but wiry, and is wearing a flannel shirt.

"Good," I say, and I think I'm going to pass out—and this close to Barr Camp. Chera sits cross-legged and stares at the two men. She's as still as the rock she sits upon and makes no expression.

"I call this Depression Rock," the pot-bellied man says. His buddy just chuckles and nods knowingly.

I don't ask why. That will take too much energy. But at least I furrow my brow—which is the same as asking, I think.

"Because from right here," says the man, "you can see where you're going." He points up high and over my head to somewhere behind me. I almost get excited, until he adds, "And it's still a long, long ways off. Kind of depressing, don't you think?"

I turn to look at where he's pointing, and so does Chera. I grunt and she winces. He's pointing to a peak high, high above us. The sun, almost even with the point of the summit, has turned it golden. And right in the center of the peak, resting on the rugged line across the horizon, I can see a teeny, tiny rectangular shape. It's a trick of the sun that makes the golden light appear to be radiating out of that little rectangular box. I look back at the man who's pointing and furrow my brow a second time, and again he seems to understand.

"That's the souvenir shop," he answers.

Chera turns from the mountain and looks at me. She's smiling. And I'm excited too, to be finally witnessing what we've talked about and planned for so many weeks. But that thrill lasts for only a moment. Because now, as I sit here, mannequin like, the depression sets in, and I think I might as well be looking at the moon: it is that far off. My back aches, my arms keep going numb because the straps on my backpack are too tight and digging into my shoulders, and my legs are telling me that they aren't going to get up and try any more today.

The two men hoist their much smaller packs onto their backs and start to go. "Hang in there," the one in the flannel shirt tells us as he scuffs his boots on the downhill. "You're just about to Barr Camp."

I can only sit and stare at the souvenir shop. Chera, however, rises from Depression Rock, her eyes on the goal, and shakes away the weariness. She wiggles into her pack. She's grinning; she's excited. "Come on, Dad. That's where we're going." And she tips her head in the direction of the peak.

I move slowly—so slowly—and think I just might die after all. I can see Tim at my funeral (breaking away from his family cookout so he can attend) saying, "I told him he could die up there, but he wouldn't listen."

All weighted down again, we step down from Depression Rock and make some more baby steps toward the top.

Just keep moving toward the top.

When I was twelve I heard that God lived in Tulsa. There was a man on television who talked about a big tower, the Prayer Tower he called it, that he'd built. And if you sent your prayers to him, just jotted them down and mailed them to the address on the television screen, he would carry them up to the top of this tower and pray for each piece of paper. I saw a picture of it on television. It was a round building high up on a pedestal, with what looked like the sun's rays shooting out from all around. But Tulsa was in another state—so far away. No matter. I was determined to get there. I stood in the kitchen, barefoot on the linoleum floor, and copied down the address. Then I found an envelope and made out my note to God. *This is such a good*

idea, I thought, as I laid the envelope and three cents in the mailbox for the postman. After that, the man from Tulsa sent me a blizzard of envelopes and paper, so it was much easier to write down my notes to God. And from what I could understand, if I sent some money along, it could only help. So the next time I folded a dollar I'd made from selling bottles and slid it in the envelope with one of my notes. Sometimes, if I'd found a lot of bottles, I'd send two dollars, sometimes only a quarter, but always something. The money would vary, but the note was always the same: *Please help Mom and Dad stop fighting and Dad to stop drinking.* I figured I'd keep sending that one over and over until God could take care of it. Time went on and I kept on sending notes, because I believed the others must have gotten lost. Or maybe it was just because the tower where God lived was just too far away. I could have used some help—at least someone to point the way.

I like it when the trail is smooth and dusty. When it's like this I only have to barely lift my feet and force them forward. The kids from the church youth group, however, don't seem to be having any problems with the grade, the elevation, or the gravity. They pass us in groups of two and three and sometimes four. "Let 'em go on past," I whisper to Chera, and we step aside and try to enjoy the breeze of their passing. "This is no race."

And people are so encouraging on the trail. It's nearly seven miles from the trailhead to Barr Camp, and we'd only been going about two miles when someone on his way down told us that we were getting close, *real close.* I guess that's the thing to do when you're on the way down: tell those you pass, who are headed up, that they're almost there. But we get used to the false hope after a few miles and stop believing everyone. We decide that most people are good intentioned or maybe just poor judges of distance—and not liars.

When we see the Barr Camp sign we want to run. Maybe in our heads we believe we are. There's barely enough daylight to snap a photo as we take turns leaning on the rusty sign. From there we follow the trail over a footbridge that spans a stream where some of the hikers (probably not the church kids) have stored bottles of beer to keep them cold. Our destination is a weathered, dark cabin with a big porch, the cabin where Fred Barr and his wife lived while he worked on the trail. I can picture them sitting on the front porch, her shelling beans for canning and him twisting dynamite fuses together for blowing up rocks later.

The Baptists have beaten us here, and most of them are sitting on benches on the porch and eating spaghetti. It smells delicious. One of the older men, a chaperone most likely, has finished his spaghetti and is playing something from the sixties on a guitar. We climb the steps to the cabin and plop our packs on the floor. Some hippies (and I don't think they'd mind this title) are serving spaghetti from a huge metal pot, using a big dipper for the sauce. A sign above the server's head tells me that a plateful will cost five dollars. Sounds like a good deal to me, but we have our own gourmet meal to prepare. So I ask the hippie where can I set up a tent, and he says anywhere that isn't taken.

"Even by the stream?" I ask.

He nods. I notice another sign that tells me that breakfast is also five dollars.

We hoist our packs one more time and leave the spaghetti to go to a flat spot by the stream, where we quickly set up the two-person tent I've been carrying all day.

"What are we going to do about supper?" Chera asks.

"We're going to make gourmet chicken teriyaki," I answer, "as soon as we build a fire."

Making the fire is easy. (We use matches.) We draw some water from the stream, plop in a couple of iodine tablets and then stir in the chicken teriyaki. At first I'm afraid there won't be enough, but then the water gets hot and the noodles swell and soon the pot is brimming with…stuff. Chera takes the first spoonful after blowing it cool. "Is it supposed to be crunchy?" she asks. This is my first campout chicken teriyaki, so I really don't know. The package doesn't tell me, so now I'm worried. We don't eat all of it. As a matter of fact, we don't eat most of it. Most of it we dump in the stream and let it wash away. We figure something in the wild will probably eat it, crunchy parts and all.

As the sun goes down, the air turns cold. We're so beat that we just brush our teeth (the cold water hurts my gums, like I knew it would) and crawl into the tent.

"What's the plan for tomorrow?" Chera asks, in the dark, in the tent.

Stay alive, I want to say. "Well, the hippie with the spaghetti said it's another six miles to the top," I begin. "If we leave early—*real early*—we might be able to beat the Baptists."

"I thought this wasn't a race," Chera says.

"Got any more aspirin?" I ask.

This could have gone much worse, I think, just before it does. A light rain begins to fall and, with muscles so sore I can hardly move, I crawl from the tent and drag in both backpacks. It's a two-person tent, barely big enough for us to stretch out. But I guess the packs help keep our feet warm and keep us from rolling down the mountain.

I am so tired. Too tired to sleep—and so I don't. I just lie there all night listening to the gurgle of the stream and the whirring of the insects in the trees and the ticking of the rain against the top of the tent. My feet and legs (and sometimes an arm) fall dead asleep, and the thousand tingling needles make me want to cry out, but I don't want to wake up Chera. She seems to be doing okay.

When the sun rises the next morning, I crawl from beneath the back-pack, from beneath the damp canvas of the tent, sore, beat, swollen, and still *tired*. I dig through my pack for more clothes, warm clothes. It's so cold today that I can see my breath whenever I moan. In only a few minutes Chera crawls out crablike from the tent, and her eyes and cheeks are red and puffy and swollen. This doesn't look right. "Can you see okay?" I ask.

She nods and touches her cheeks. "Yeah, why? My eyes feel a little sore and—oh, it's so cold!" She hugs herself and then races to her backpack, try-ing not to trip over her untied bootlaces, and pulls out a sweater. I fish out ten dollars from my wallet and say, "Let's go see what's for breakfast."

"You don't even look like yourself," she tells me as we walk to the cabin. I haven't looked in a mirror yet, but I can imagine.

"I don't feel like it either," I say.

After a tall stack of pecan pancakes, we pull together daypacks, which are just small backpacks stuffed with an extra sweatshirt and some food for later. We leave the heavy stuff in the tent for now; we'll pick it up on the way down. It's still early, only seven, when we hit the trail, and lots of the church kids are still eating when we begin to climb. It's still cold enough to see your breath, and the only warm places are those little spots where sun-light breaks through the trees in sunny patches. We've only hiked about a quarter of a mile when we stop and Chera tells me, "Okay, I tried, but I think I'm really going to need it." I know what she's talking about because she mentioned it just before we stopped. We're resting in a warm patch of sunshine, letting the yellow light draw the puffiness from our eyes. Now she squints into the sun and twists her face in a way that says to me, *Sorry about that.*

I take a deep breath, and everything I want to say—like, *Are you sure? I mean, how bad can it be? I'm sure lots of women climb this mountain with-out bras*—sticks in my throat. Her twisted-up, apologetic face causes me to blow out all those misstatements in a thin fog that the sun quickly burns away. And, instead of sounding like Jerk of the Mountain—which would have been easy—I simply say, "Okay." And we turn around and hike back down to camp. We smile at the youth group as they head up past us in the other direction.

Once we (Chera, mainly) are fully outfitted, we head back up. We hike on for a mile, then two, through the thick green and brown forest, in and out of mottled patches of sunlight, the smell of cold pine needles in my sinuses now, stopping from time to time to rest and to view the heavy fog lifting from the valley to expose the quaint town of Manitou Springs (where the train depot is). This high up, the giant trees we once ambled through have now turned dwarflike, having lived the bulk of their lives in the path of a heavy, twisting gale. I imagine the lives of these gnarled and stunted trees, clinging to the mountain as sheer winds constantly sweep the peak clean. Rather than rise tall and spread thick and green like those that surrounded the parking lot far, far below us, these trees send all their strength and mass downward to the roots, finding a powerful purchase in the thin soil and cracks of the stones. There's a lesson in there somewhere, but just now I don't have the energy to think of what it is. After three miles we break above the tree line, and the view is bright and glorious—and so bright! Did I say bright?

We're at nearly twelve thousand feet and already higher than many of the peaks around us. The city below is nothing more than pinpoints of sunlight reflected back to us off building roofs and cars and small lakes. The fog lifts and forms big fluffy clouds that are slowly moving away to reveal a sky as blue as Kool-Aid. The wind threatens to sweep us away, so we hunker down a bit to make ourselves smaller, like the trees have done. We can only trust that our boots won't fail us now.

Through a series of switchbacks, reminiscent of the beginning of the trail, we work back and forth across the great stark and rocky face of this mountain (the bald ridge that had reminded me of my high-school history teacher's head). High above us we see tiny figures, and we guess that's where we have to go. We haven't been able to see the souvenir shop since Depression Rock, and that's sort of depressing. We aren't exactly sure, even with our twenty-five-cent map, where it is we're heading—besides up, of course. When we look up, we don't know which craggy peak is ours.

We stop to eat some lunch—tuna fish and crackers—on a sun-drenched rock. While we eat we watch tiny people climbing up from below. "Look how far we've come," I say to Chera as I point out over the rocky grade. We can see the zigzagging line of the trail spanning far below us. We could be viewing the town from an airplane.

As we rest and eat our tuna fish, a man who looks like Santa Claus hikes toward us quickly, his eyes glued to the trail, his thumbs hitched in the straps of his backpack. He's wearing a pair of light-colored shorts, and his legs are white and wiry, *like goat legs,* I think. A ball cap covers most of his head, but long white tufts of hair stick out around the edges, and his beard is full and snowy white. When he reaches us, he stops and says hello. He wears round glasses, making his eyes look bigger than they are. "Beautiful day for a climb, isn't it?" he says. We make small talk for a bit, and then Chera asks him, "Have you ever climbed this mountain before?"

He grins—just like Santa—and says, "Thirty-three times. This will be thirty-four. I hope to hit fifty before I stop."

Stop? What does he mean by that? Retire? Move on to a different mountain? But I know what he means: he means before he dies. That's his plan. He's at least in his sixties now. *Can it be done? Is there time?* I'm glad I'm not saying any of this out loud. But I'm sure the pause is giving me away. It's been such a long pause since he's said the word "stop." We try to cover up our thoughts (my thoughts) by praising him. And even though we're sincere, it's obvious these praises are in lieu of something tasteless like, *Well, well, you'd better get crackin', old man, because at your age...* Our new friend takes it all with a smile and wishes us well on this, our first climb. He adjusts his pack and moves on up the trail with all the strength and agility of a mountain goat.

Much later Chera and I trudge along, far from goatlike, covering only about one mile every hour. The trail markers are such that they count down to the top, like a blastoff. Four. Three. Two. And when we reach the one-mile marker, we stop to take more pictures. The view never falters below glorious, but what catches my attention at this stop is the man on his cellular phone. "Yeah, I'm about a mile from the top," he says into his little flip-open phone. "Oh no, the weather's gorgeous… Yeah, lots of pictures… No, no need to send the helicopter. Looks like we're going to make it." I want to make that same call too. We're only a mile from the top. We've come nearly twelve miles so far. We're going to make it! I wonder if there's a name for right now, for this exact, precise moment when your heart teams up with your head and demands that your arms, legs, back, and feet quit their whining. Forget about it, forget about all the pain and ache—it's not about you now: *It's all about the top. The top is there. Got to make it to the top!* I think maybe there are two words, and they go together: *reckless abandon.* We're excited, but we still have to be careful.

Chera takes this time to rework her ponytail. She pulls her hair back tighter and twists it with a rubber band into a neat, tiny knot at the crown of her head. This reminds me of the scene in *Rambo* when Sylvester Stallone ties a bandanna around his forehead. Chera is Rambo and her face says, *Let's take this mountain!* I follow her and the best we can do is baby step upward, always upward. For a long time we can still hear the man on the cell phone chatting, roaming most likely.

Our friends at Depression Rock the day before had told us that the last mile is the toughest, and now we're finding that out. The grade is much steeper; shoot, the grade is straight up and down, like walking up a wall! The rocks are bigger, and sometimes we have to grab hold of a slick, well-worn edge and pull ourselves up and over. I think that old Fred Barr must have run out of money and dynamite right here at the top and couldn't blow these rocks to pebbles like he had the others. The trail is so sheer now that we can't see much at all of what's ahead, but we can see everything that lies below us. We stop at another marker to breathe. The metal sign beside us reads 16 Golden Stairs.

"What does that mean?" Chera asks.

I shrug. "I don't know." We see other hikers not too far above us, moving upward, but also going back and forth in shorter stretches now, as if pacing the floor. "Switchbacks," I guess. "Maybe the stairs are switchbacks and there are sixteen of them." I give Chera a big smile. "We're close, Chera. We are *so* close." *There are sixteen stairs from the living room of my house to the upstairs office,* I think. Just pretend I'm climbing up for my car keys. But Chera has a better idea.

"Okay," she begins and then pauses, and I can see she's turning something over in her head. "So there are sixteen stairs. Let's do at least four before we rest. That's four sets of four, and then we'll be at the top. How does that sound?"

The math sounds all right to me. I wish it were all about math. We take a drink. We take some aspirin. And I lead the way for the first set of four. I learn right away that *stairs* is a misnomer. These sections—some only about ten yards long, others maybe a hundred yards—are nearly straight up, like ladders. After the first set of four, I crash onto the rocks and wheeze. "Killer!" I croak through a parched throat.

"Are you okay, Dad?" Chera asks. (We've been asking each other this since we started at the wrong trailhead over twenty-four hours before.)

"Fine," I croak.

When I can finally breathe through my nose—and not my mouth—I stand up and lead the charge for the second run of four. And since what would be the first leg of the next section appears to be so short, we cheat and take it in too. We crash again and take even longer to rest this time.

Most of the church group has passed us by, but after all, I remind myself, we aren't racing. We do four more stairs, then four more, and the stairs don't stop. We do four more and still no summit. We're resting and breathing hard and reworking the math when we see Goat Man making his way down. There's a twinkle in his eye and he's grinning. "You're doing great," he says. "You're nearly there. Not very far at all." He keeps walking down.

"Congratulations on number thirty-four!" Chera calls to him, and he half turns and smiles and thanks her. He looks as if he might say something like, "And look for something special under your tree this year." But he just turns and keeps walking. That's what you do on this mountain: keep walking.

We lose count of the stairs, but we've lost faith in our math, anyway.

At one point Chera and I stand with our backs to the mountain, leaning against the rock. Resting. "Hey, Chera," I say between breaths. "Remember that live video feed you found on the Internet?"

"Yeah."

And I begin to wave to nothing but the azure sky and the tiny, faraway city where car bumpers still reflect the sun. "Chera. Wave to Mom," I say. "Wave to your brother, Zachary," I say as I wave my arm in big loopy arcs. We both do. (I wish I'd told Chonda and Zach about that Web site so they could really see this and we wouldn't have to pretend.) But the waving is taking too much energy, so we stop and just breathe hard. "We're close," I tell Chera. And I wonder how many times I've said that today, in the last hour, even. She grins, probably because she's done the math and knows.

"Wow, this is incredible!" I hear someone say. I crane my head upward and can see two upside-down faces looking down at us and then back up at the scenery that surrounds us. *Tourists!* I think suddenly. They've probably ridden to the top by car or train and then strolled down from the souvenir shop to take a peek over the edge. They're close enough I could hit them with a rock (not that I want to, and besides, I've used up all my energy waving at the camera).

"Chera," I say, almost in a whisper, as if I'm hiding from the tourists. "There's the top! Those people are standing at the top!"

Now she turns her head slowly, tilts it all the way back, her short ponytail dropping between her shoulder blades. "Yes!" she rasps, and seems to come alive as she pumps her small fist in the air like she does whenever she comes alive.

Her life gives me life. "Let's take it to the top and not stop until we get there," I say, thinking I sound like a smarmy hero in a B movie. Chera only nods. Not having seen many B movies in her short lifetime, maybe to her I sound original.

I push away from our rock and start up whatever number golden stair this happens to be. The pain in my calves and upper legs comes back just as quickly. *To the top! To the top! To the top!* my head and heart chant as one. I glance back and see Chera right behind me, only a step away. When we turn the corner of the last switchback, I see the tourists fully, and I can also see that they aren't exactly at the top. They've hiked a good five hundred feet from the souvenir shop, all uphill from here (*I can still hit them with a rock,* I think), but we can't stop now. Besides, there are no more big rocks to lean on: we're in an open, rocky field somewhere near the summit.

I look back at Chera, trying to hide the panic that I'm feeling because I've just discovered that we still have more to climb, and I'm not sure I have it in me. Then I see it. Our inspiration. "Look!" I shout and point. "It's the souvenir shop!" With our daypacks resting at our feet, I fall in beside her and place an arm around her shoulders. It's impossible to tell who's helping whom the most as together we walk toward the plain rectangular building that someone's probably staring at right now from far below, at Depression Rock. "Got to make it a little farther," I say. Now my legs are noodles, and Chera's pained expression seems to indicate it's at least that bad for her.

The closer we get to the souvenir shop, the more tourists we have to push through. Scores of people, most wearing heavy jackets, are everywhere, scattered about the edges of the summit, gazing off into the blue and green and haze. Many are snapping pictures and pointing to things you really can't make out from this high up. We stop at a big sign made of plywood that reads Pikes Peak Summit 14,110 ft. I take a picture of it. Then Chera and I ask a man, who must be nearly eighty, to take our picture together. We pose by raising a triumphant fist in the air. My shoulder aches, and I silently pray for the man to hurry.

As Chera and I stand there, frozen for the camera, the sun so bright and the wind so brisk that it makes my eyes water, I suddenly have this incredible feeling, and I think I know why. I think it's because I can't go any higher—it would be impossible to (unless, of course, we try to climb this plywood sign we're standing next to, which seems neither a safe nor sane thing to do). For two days we've pushed upward through such a heavy canopy of gravity. For so far and so long we didn't seem to be going anywhere, just back and forth. Then, with the same routine we started the climb with (a wobbly, unsure step), we placed foot onto the summit, where all things around us—in every direction—are tiny and far away. And that's only part of the feeling. The best thing is that the canopy, once so heavy, is all gone now, and although our feet have never left the ground, we're flying!

"So how did *you* get up here?" I ask the gentleman who snapped our picture as I wipe the water (a tear, from the wind) from the corner of one eye with the back of my hand. I don't really care to know, but I'm hoping he'll ask me the same thing.

He hands me my camera and says, "Me and the wife took the train. How about you?"

There it is! I pause for effect, look to Chera and say, "We"—and I circle a finger to indicate Chera and myself—"walked." *(Maybe I should have said "climbed," I think immediately, or even "hiked.")* But the man is still amazed. And the look on his face is worth it all—the aching legs, the stabbing pain in the lungs, the parched throat and cracked lips, the swollen fingers that hurt whenever I make a fist. Chera must think so too, because she's beaming, glowing, nodding. But have we really done all this—climb a mountain—just to impress an old man who took a train?

We go inside the souvenir shop and buy some T-shirts for ourselves, a pocketknife for Zachary, and a ball cap for Chonda. Then we each eat a giant cheeseburger (this was better than the simple ice-cream cone I'd wanted at first) before heading back down the trail, with lighter spirits, fuller bellies, and elated hearts.

Going down is so easy that it feels like we're gliding, sliding, falling. We feel so good now that we search for the proper way to express our elation whenever we pass someone who's on his or her way up. One gentleman, who appears to be a bit confused, is resting about halfway up the Golden Stairs and is using his fingers and thumbs like they're an abacus. "You're close," I say, trying to be an encouragement.

"You're *real* close," Chera adds. We do that a lot on the way back to Barr Camp.

That evening at camp, and just before the sun can go down and the cold can return for the night, we sit by a small fire that we feed twigs into. I find a scripture in Psalms that I'd discovered weeks before but was saving for this time. I want to read it to Chera, now that we've actually climbed a mountain. I'd been saving it for such a time as this. So I sit on soft pine needles next to our small tent by the small stream with the small fire blazing and read in the thin air:

His lightning lights up the world; the earth sees and trembles. The mountains melt like wax before the LORD, before the Lord of all the earth. (Psalm 97:4–5)

"Isn't that incredible?" I ask. "You've been to the top of a real mountain now," I add. "Can you imagine the awesome power of a God who can melt this thing"—and I stamp the ground with my foot *(ouch!)*—"as if it were wax?" I'm just trying to find a way to recognize the majesty and awesomeness of God, an awesomeness that can't be denied, especially after where we'd just been. An awesomeness that makes everything and every problem around us seem small, like looking at your troubles from the top of Pikes Peak. Chera just nods and accepts these words about God without much comment. But then again, she always seems to do that. The truth seems to hit her heart like a seed pushed deep into fertile soil, where it's instantly watered and cultivated. Grows. In a few weeks, I even expect she'll be quoting this verse as if it were her favorite. For now, it is I who stand (in this case, *sit*) amazed by the wonders of God. I hadn't expected this, not in this way, this powerfully. I read those words over and over and soak them in myself. *Melt like wax.* What an awesome power!

Chera, however, has to sing.

The next day (after another night of listening to the babbling brook and cantankerous crickets; at least it didn't rain) we stuff our packs, big and heavy, eat breakfast (compliments of the hippies) with the Baptists, and move down from Barr Camp. We've gone maybe five hundred feet when Chera says, "I forgot my rocks."

"What rocks?" I want to know. And how could you forget a rock with so many reminders everywhere?

"The rocks I took from the peak. My souvenirs," she says.

I want to tell her to just borrow her mother's souvenir hat, but instead I tell her to stay put and I'll go back. I make a big circle and turn around on the trail. Up the familiar path I go. Pain and déjà vu make me dizzy. I make it back to Barr Camp and then find the even skinnier footpath to our campsite, and there, at the base of the tree she had described, is a pile of three small stones. I kneel down and lift them, using my legs and not my back. I'm suddenly glad I came back. Here are three of Fred Barr's rocks, to forever hold, and finger, and remember.

I glide back down and catch up with Chera, and together we go down the mountain. We haven't gone very far when Chera suddenly says, "Let's sing praise choruses."

"Okay," I say, but with less enthusiasm. I'm not a singer. But at least now we aren't fighting for every breath like we had been on the way up. "I like that one about the mountains," I say.

She's not sure which one I'm talking about. So I try to sing a little: "You know, *Over the oceans and the hills*—"

"No, no," she interrupts, laughing. "It's *Over the mountains and the sea...*"

I know even less of the rest of the verses. But when we get to the chorus, we sing and sing, just like the song says: *"I could sing of your love forever. I could sing of your love forever."*

We pass some people who are on their way up, and I stop singing. But Chera keeps on. She even cuts a hard glance at me over her shoulder, as if to say, *How dare you stop singing in such a glorious place?* "Sing, Dad!" she says on a rest beat.

So I try: *"I could sing of your love*—You guys are doing great! You're almost there!—*forever. I could sing of your love forever."*

Before we get to the bottom, my shins begin to hurt. They feel like someone's just whacked them with a baseball bat. Shin splints. I'd heard of them but never had them. Now I do. I hobble the rest of the way. At the bottom of the mountain there's no fanfare for us. Just like there hadn't been at the top. We pass lots of tourists, lots of people taking their pictures by the Barr Trail sign, lots of people buying tickets for the train that will take them all the way to the top. It's been two and a half days since we first sat here, only a few feet away, and ate our sandwiches. Chera walks and I hobble about a mile into town, where we catch a cab that takes us back to the airport.

As we ride, the mountain moves around us, from the passenger side of the car to the rear window to the driver's window. We watch it circle around like a big moon across the sky. We take turns closing one eye and squinting the other nearly shut and reaching to the glass and pointing to the peak gingerly, as if it could prick our fingers, and saying, "Right there. *Right there* is where we were."

Nearly to the airport we can see the whole mountain, the green that washes up at its base like a sea—or a tuft of hair—the big craggy, rocky expanse of its face (that still reminds me of my history teacher's head), and finally, the crooked peak where there stands a little souvenir shop in which visitors can purchase a memory for a few bucks. But nothing they can purchase there will tell them anything about Encyclopedia Man, or pecan pancakes, or crunchy teriyaki chicken, or Goat Man, who still has sixteen more climbs before he "stops," or the fleet-footed Baptists, or the sixteen Golden Stairs, or the lyrics to a song I can never remember.

In the cab, on the way to the airport, we are so sore, so tired, so beat, and so swollen; and when I say we are changed, it doesn't have anything to do with any of that. I think about Goat Man, who just keeps walking. I think about how excited Chera got when we saw the summit from Depression Rock. I think about how, for two days, we moved up, always toward the top, no matter how tired or beat. I'm proud of Chera for making sure we had all the right supplies (I take blame for the chicken teriyaki), for bringing aspirin that kept us from drowning, for pushing and pulling me, and for the talks—I haven't forgotten the talks.

It's over. We did it. Now we can rest while we ride to the airport.

Over the years I must have written hundreds of notes to God and sent them to Tulsa. I imagined the man on television carrying them up the steps of the Prayer Tower in a knapsack. A bulging bag that caused him to hunch over. I imagined God busily rifling through the mail, stacking and ordering and saying, "Yes, yes, let me put this one on top. The kid's going to get writer's cramp if I don't do something soon." Because I could imagine a scene like this, I kept on writing. But over the years, the prayer went unanswered. I came to believe God wasn't in Tulsa. I didn't know where he was.

After graduating high school, my best friend and I headed to Colorado to camp out for a week. For several days we drove through the mountains without any particular plan. Passed by Pikes Peak. Slept beneath the stars. Lived close to heaven for a whole week.

On the way back he wanted to visit a good friend—who lived in Tulsa. "While you're here," this friend told us, "you have to go see the Prayer Tower. It's the only thing to see in Tulsa." I went along, although I didn't tell them my story about the Prayer Tower. Nor did I tell them that I still knew the mailing address by heart, even though I hadn't written any notes for years. I didn't tell them that at one time I'd kept the old man busy going up and down those steps with dollars and prayers. We went to the gift shop, but for some reason we didn't go in the tower like we could have. But I remember standing in a garden, near the base of the tower, and looking up at the round structure anchored high up at the peak of tower, the sun glistening off the windows and the row of points that looked like rays of sunshine. *All that glass. All that concrete,* I thought. *And the thing doesn't even work.* No. I didn't find God there in Tulsa. But that wasn't going to keep me from looking. From climbing.

Chera wants to know what we're going to do next. "We'll have to check our backpacks and get our boarding passes," I say.

"No," she says. "I mean *after* that. What's our *next* adventure?" Was she really already planning and preparing something else?

I haven't thought about a next adventure. I'm so sore now I can hardly move. Things (joints) are setting up like mortar. But I'm thinking, *Yeah, I guess we can do something.* Like Goat Man—we'll just keep walking. (...*before we stop?* Why did I have to think *that* part?) But I'll think more about our next adventure later. Right now I have to take a few minutes to catch my breath. Right now, as we move farther from the mountain, I'm trying to figure out what I should do about this nineteen-year-old boy she likes.

3

We Run
a Good Race

We hold hands as we finish
our first marathon.

W e're back home in middle Tennessee, far from any zigzaggy trails that lead to craggy peaks. Chera's just fine. All she needed was a good night's rest and she was ready for school the next day. She wore her new T-shirt that reads Got Oxygen? and told all her friends about how we'd made it to the top and back down again without drowning. But me...*I've* got to get help. Professional help. It's been a week since we climbed Pikes Peak, and I'm still hurting.

I have what I think are normal hurts—arms, legs, feet; I can deal with those. But then there are these strange hurts, hurts I'm almost embarrassed to mention. The fronts of my legs, just below the knees, are killing me. When I walk it's as if a tiny, invisible person is whacking me with something hard at every step. And that's not all. My shoulders are aching, for sure, but so are my armpits! (I'm most embarrassed about this.) When I put my hands on my head, like I'm just waking up and stretching the sleep away, it's better, but I know I can't do this all day. I don't think mountain climbers should hurt like this. I need some help. So I do something I've never done before in my life: I join a gym—Gold's Gym even, where guys walk around in shirts too small for them, and they have bench-pressing championships every other week. If I'm going to keep up with Chera, I've got to get in shape.

"Can you help me?" I say to the young man behind the counter. Close by is a display of legal supplements that promise to make your arms as big as trees. The aroma of wet cotton and musk surrounds me and can't be fanned away. The young man's name is Eric, and he's my "after" photo. I want the big arms (guns), little waist, and giant chest like his. I'm ready to cut and paste.

"Want to muscle up?" he asks me above the clanging of iron against iron. Basically I just want to tone up; that was my plan when I walked in the door. But when Eric offers me muscle, I change my mind. This is the muscle I wanted back in high school but couldn't have because I was ninety-eight pounds total then—bones, skin, teeth, hair, sneakers, all of it. Ninety-eight pounds. I was on the wrestling team and got whipped by lots of other ninety-eight-pounders. (The next year I got whipped by a bunch of hundred-and-five-pounders.) So now Eric's giving me a chance to be a muscle man, and I say, "Why not?"

Eric nods. He knows my type.

"Let's see where you are," he says, and with clipboard and pencil in hand, he leads me to a scale and asks me to step on. He stores the pencil in his mouth and uses his free hand to tap the scale's counterweight farther and farther across the band until the pointer floats in the little rectangular opening. "Looks like one seventy-two," he says, and he writes that down. Then he leads me across the floor to the bench-press machine, and I follow him, one hand resting self-consciously on my belly. Eric sets the weight to a hundred pounds. (That's me in high school!) "Okay," he says, stepping back to give me room. "Just lie here"—he points to the bench—"and pump that to failure so I can check your form."

This doesn't take long. I fail at six times. "So how'd I look?" I pant.

He shakes his head, a bit uncertain. "I'm not sure. I didn't see enough."

"Sorry." I mop my sweaty brow with the tail of my T-shirt. "I can probably do another one."

He makes a check mark on the clipboard. "That's okay. You'll get stronger," he promises.

Maybe I should have worked out in secret before coming here. You know, lift weights at night while everyone slept—stealth exercise. Then I could come in here all muscled up and Eric would say, "Looks like you're finished. There's nothing here we can improve on." *But then again,* I think, *I'm the kind of person this place is for.* This place, this noisy, smelly gym, is where I start. *Here* is where I can grow strong.

Eric's seen enough and sets me up on a beginner's program, which starts with a few minutes each time on the treadmill. There are six treadmills here, and all are facing three television sets hanging from metal brackets fastened to the ceiling. One set is tuned to bizarre music videos (it's best not to watch these equilibrium-affecting videos while you're trying to run on a treadmill), another to a sports channel, and the last to an all-news channel. I try to watch all three as I settle into a nice, brisk walking pace. Back and forth, back and forth I watch. Already my neck is feeling stronger.

Weeks go by; my pace picks up. Sometimes Chera goes with me, and we run and work out together. I'm feeling much stronger all over now, armpits included. I read somewhere that when older people discover exercise, they believe they've experienced an epiphany. I slap my forehead and think, *So that's what's happened,* because I'm really enjoying myself now. Then something happens that causes me to start dreading the treadmill. Every morning a woman with big, big thighs and wearing neon spandex takes the machine next to me and changes the sports channel to *Little House on the Prairie.* Then she turns up the volume so loud that everyone on this end of the gym can hear it, and then she hides the remote control in her cup holder so no one can get to it. This goes on for a couple of weeks. Sometimes, if I finish treadmilling before the episode is over, I'll worry about Charles and Caroline Ingalls all day.

I'm taking a water break one morning, wondering if Charles is going to lose the farm or if his friends will all pull together and help him pay his debts, at least until the crops can come in. (When they did this before I almost cried; the woman in spandex did.) But before I can worry too much, I notice a brochure pinned to the bulletin board there by the water fountain. It's an advertisement for the very first Country Music Marathon in Nashville, with the promise of a different live country music band at every mile. The race would take place only six weeks from now, at the end of April. *There's no way in the world I'd even try that,* I think.

Only a few hours later I'm in the car with the family when I tell Chera, "I ran two miles today. That's a first."

Chera claps. "That's great, Dad!" she says. I'm proud that she's proud of me.

She asks about today's *Little House on the Prairie,* and I have to tell her that Charles is losing the farm—again. As I re-create the moments of the morning, I remember the brochure on the corkboard by the water fountain. "And I read about a marathon going on next month in Nashville," I tell her and everyone in the car. "A marathon! Wouldn't that be tough?" I shake my head, smiling sourly, as if I'm saying no to the windshield.

It's Chonda who speaks next. And for a brief but all-important moment, my life unfolds like a *Little House on the Prairie* episode, the one where Caroline Ingalls finishes darning Charles's shirt and hands it back to her husband and asks, "We're staying on the prairie, aren't we? Even though the drought killed the crops, the wolves ate the cattle, Mary's going blind, and Laura could use some orthodontic work that you can only find in the big city—we are staying, aren't we?" And Charles Ingalls takes his freshly darned shirt, tears up (always tears up), nods (and his perfect mane just bounces), and says, "Sure. Of course we're staying." What he doesn't tell Caroline is that he's already got the horses hitched to the wagon for a quick escape from the prairie—until he realizes how much staying means to her. He stays teared up and they—Charles, Caroline, Laura, and Mary—group hug right there in the big room of the one-room cabin. Later, discreetly, he slips out and unhitches the wagon.

But my wife…in the car sitting next to me on the way to town (my biceps no larger than the day I received my Gold's Gym membership card four months before), says, "You guys are running in it, aren't you?" The excitement in her voice does me in. I'm feeling very Charles Ingalls–like. I glance at Chera and she glances back at me, much like we had that day at the Pikes Peak trailhead when we knew that with the very next step the adventure officially began, and I say, "Sure, of course we are. Right, Chera?"

Now Chera's eyes light up. She hears and smells adventure. And she says, "That'd be awesome, Dad! Wow! Running in a marathon!" The car gets quiet, and I know it's time for a group hug, only we're in a car and not a one-room cabin.

Chera breaks the silence. "So how far is a marathon anyway?"

"Twenty-six-point-two miles," I answer, as if I'm talking to the windshield.

More silence. Slow tearing up. No hugs. I ran two miles just earlier this morning, my personal best. I sense a dark, scary storm blowing in from the far horizon, but I've already unhitched the horses.

"Point two?" says Zachary, who is nine. "Why don't they just make it an even twenty-six?"

Yeah, I think. *An even twenty-six. That'd be so much better.*

Frank Shorter is the first thing I think of when I think *marathon*. I saw him on television once, during the Olympics, when I was a kid. It was July 1976. I remember this because my dad and I were living in a small house trailer, next to a river. I'd just gotten my driver's license a couple months before. We had an old black-and-white television set (not because there were no color televisions back then, but because Dad and me had left home—where there was a real nice color television—to start life on our own). I remember pulling up in the driveway, coming back from my friend's house, and walking in to the sound of people cheering and the voice of a commentator describing the scene, which was a nicety for us, because on our scratchy black-and-white set you couldn't always be sure of what you were seeing.

"Boy, that guy can run," Dad said (he'd been drinking), pointing to the snowy picture. The picture improved as I walked across the floor. I stopped at an instant of clarity and watched a man slight of stature, wearing a tank top and teeny shorts, loping through the streets of some big city—Montreal, I think. "That's that Frank Shorter everyone's been talking about," Dad continued. He knew everyone was talking about him because he'd been watching the Olympics steadily for the last few days (better than the daily soap operas) and keeping me posted on America's growing collection of gold. "Mark Spitz won again," he told me. But I was watching the thin man run. He was soaked with sweat and water. People—thousands of people—formed a lane for him to run through. And from the edges they held out cups of water, and he'd snatch one from a loose grip and gulp part of it and splash the rest on his face. People were clapping and cheering and waving him on. I watched this for maybe a minute before the scene suddenly switched to the pole vault competition or something. Then I stepped away and the clarity was gone, but I don't think Dad noticed.

And that's all I know about running a marathon: small shorts and water.

"What about training?" Chera asks me one day.

"Training?" My response is heavy with doubt and ignorance, but mainly ignorance.

"Yeah. I talked to my track coach, and he says there's a schedule we should keep up with, so that by the time the race comes, we're running up to twenty miles a day."

I don't like the idea of this at all. I figure if I'm going to run twenty-six miles, it'll be a one-time thing. (I can't do it over and over.) And if by chance I drop dead somewhere around the twenty-mile marker, I want to save it for race day—so I'll be with thousands who are clapping and holding water cups and taking pictures (probably of me falling into the water table)—not alone on the side of the road, discovered days later by a road crew mowing. "So how do we do that?" I ask Chera about the training.

"I'm not sure."

"I say we just run some every day, and on race day, we just run slower and longer. I mean, it's all the same thing—just more of it. How hard can that be?" Chera goes along with this.

She practices at school with the track team. During meets she runs the mile in about ten minutes. Not real fast, but she always finishes. And I practice in the mornings, in the neighborhood. I jog to the supermarket and back for a round-trip total of two miles. Sometimes I run fast, sometimes slow (especially if I get caught by the crossing guard at the school). When I'm back in my front yard, I multiply that pain by thirteen and try to imagine how I'm going to feel after twenty-six miles. I'm worried.

And then we find Tiger Hill, which in an otherwise flat neighborhood, is not hard to do. Only two miles from the house is the tallest hill in the county. I know this because one day while I was jogging down (after dragging myself up), a county sheriff patrolman pulled up beside me in his car and called from his window, "Well, you picked the highest hill in the county to run up, didn't you?" I think I smiled, tried to anyway.

The most impressive thing about Tiger Hill is that it hits you from out of nowhere. Almost Mount Rainier–like (volcano-like). Some other hills, smaller hills, surround it, and tall trees feather around its base, but nothing can take away from its impressive, jolting "tallness." A single road that you can't see until you're directly in front of it leads to the top. From this head-on look at the road, steep and narrow and void of switchbacks, I'm reminded of a monster ski chute: the Agony of Defeat.

The first time I ever tackled Tiger Hill, I was trying to ride my bike up one morning. I threw up, and then I lay down right in the middle of the street, next to my bicycle. *Just bust it going up,* I thought. *Give it all you got. You can rest coming down.* But only a quarter of the way up, my legs stopped working. For all the money in the world (a game I like to play), I could not will them to make another rotation, nor could I will them to step off and stand on the firm ground that now angled up sharply at no less than forty-five degrees. All I could do was stand on the pedals, balancing the bike there in the middle of the road. No longer was my energy invested in trying to go forward; now it was fully devoted to preventing what would surely be a devastating roll backward. So I did the only thing I could do with the body parts that still functioned: I tipped myself over. I went down softly (considering it was a paved road). But I was so glad to relax, to feel the flow of blood back into my legs, arms, head—and what was that taste? Spaghetti? I'd had that for supper the night before. I pulled myself from underneath the bike. *No, wait. I need to set up the kickstand first,* I thought. Because if someone drives by, he'll see me lying here (probably with spaghetti on my shirt), and if he doesn't freak out or crash into the woods, he'll call the rescue team. How embarrassing would that be? So I stood up and set the bike on its stand (a big "I'm okay, really" sign) and then lay out on the street and wished I were dead. A man in a van pulled up beside me and rolled down his window.

"I tried that once!" he called out.

I swallowed and nodded.

"Of course, the scariest part is going down. You only have two real skinny pieces of rubber holding you back." He pinched his thumb and forefinger to about a half inch just to show me how skinny a brake is. "Well, hey, be careful," he said and drove away. I lay down again on the asphalt and felt the warmth of the sun coming up through the pavement and cooking me on the back—like a grill. This...this *cooking* seemed to settle my stomach. Before long I made myself get up, and then I pushed the bike the rest of the way to the top. The ride down was nothing but fun.

That night I told Chera about Tiger Hill and that we had to do this together, as part of the training. "If you survive Tiger Hill," I told her, "then a marathon is nothing." Of course, I said that like I actually knew what I was talking about.

It is a sunny spring morning in April, three weeks before the race, when I set out for my run to the supermarket parking lot, only this time, when I get to the school where I usually make the turn for the supermarket, I go the other way, toward a park. Earlier I clocked this route at three and a half miles. I lope down the sidewalk, ready for this. Only when I get back to the house (after running the farthest I've ever run), I don't stop. I do it again. The whole way. Seven miles total now. Then I do a Forrest Gump sort of thing and run it again. Ten miles! I should have grabbed some water along the way, but I was in the zone. Ten miles! And before I can celebrate too much, a voice reminds me, *Now double that and then tack on another six-point-two miles.* I'm still worried.

That night the pain—excruciating, killing, ragged—sets in. It starts in my heels, claws its way up my ankles, twists its way around to my shins, and then needles its way back down into the tips of my toes. I want to cry, but I don't. "I'll be okay," I tell Chera as I prop my feet up on all the pillows from the couch and a couple from the bedroom. "Maybe I need more arch support."

For three days I hobble around. I can see that Chera is concerned about my not being able to walk too well, but I can also tell she's worried that the race is over for us. I know that look so well that I could draw it if I had to, and I don't even have any skills as an artist. I can't stand to disappoint her like this, so I decide to get more professional help.

"I need some running shoes," I tell the young clerk at the shoe store. He shows me a pair of white sneakers with orange stripes down the side. "Can you run in these?" I ask.

"You can run in army boots if you want to, man," he says with a country twang.

"What I mean is, do these have good arch support?"

The kid takes one of the shoes out of the box. He clutches the toe in one hand and the heel in the other and gives it a good bend and twist. "Yeah," he says. "These are real nice."

"A good shoe ought to twist and bend like that?" I ask, taking the shoe from him and studying it myself. "That's a good test?" I don't know.

"They're on sale," he answers.

I give the shoe my own twist and bend and say, "I'll take 'em."

Guess I was right about the nineteen-year-old: he does like Chera. Only now he's twenty and Chera is sixteen. She's driving and we've given her permission to date—only not twenty-year-olds. Brad calls the house one night, looking for Chera. I answer the phone.

Brad: Is Chera there?

Me: Brad?

Brad: Yeah.

Me: I need to talk to you for a minute.

Brad: Yeah?

Me: You're twenty. Chera's sixteen. I don't think it's a good idea that you two get too friendly.

Brad: (Silence)

Me: I'm not saying you can never call her again—or that you can't be her friend. I'm just saying it's not a good idea to spend a lot of time with her. Since you're twenty and she's sixteen.

Brad: (Silence)

Me: Do you understand what I'm saying?

Brad: Yeah, I understand.

Me: (Silence)

Brad: (Silence)

Me: Well, good night.

Brad: Good night.

That went pretty well. My wife thought I was magnificent.

I'm in Houston with Chonda. My wife is a comedian and she's working tonight, trying to make people laugh, when Chera calls me on the cell phone. I'm in a big arena with lots of people around, and the buzz of conversation is more like a roar. But I can still hear my daughter's pained and broken voice.

"Dad?"

My heart stops and parks itself right there in my throat. It's not going to beat again until I'm sure she's all right. "Chera?" And in that one word— her name—I'm asking her to tell me that she's all right, that nothing's broken, that nothing's bleeding. *Answer me and answer me fast.*

"I just went to Wal-Mart," she says. *That means she was on the interstate in her car,* I think. *Or she could have taken the back roads. But at least she's talking to me now. She's okay. Unless, of course, she's pinned in and just managed to punch the speed dial on her phone and mine is the number she found. What if that's the case? Or what if she's hurt really badly? What if they had to airlift her to the hospital? And what if she made it to the hospital only to be held up in triage because she can't supply administration with the proper insurance information? What if that's what she's doing now—holding her severed leg in one hand and the cell phone in the other, about to ask me for a policy number?* I reach for my wallet when she says, "And someone there told me that Elizabeth Jones was killed last night."

So Chera's okay.

"Is this someone you know?" This is a stupid thing to say.

"A little," she says. She's crying. "She sat next to me in English class. I didn't talk to her that much."

I could hear regret in her voice. Chera sat next to her in class, saw her every day at school, yet she never got to tell her about the love of God— because that's what Chera does: tells people about God. She's grieving for the girl she knew, but really didn't know; she's grieving for the girl's soul. I know some kids want to be like their parents. I want to be more like my daughter.

"I'm so sorry, Chera. That is so hard. Are you with someone now?"

The sitter is there. And even though Chera is sixteen and hates the fact that we hired a sitter to stay with her and Zach, she's glad she's there this night. Chonda is somewhere in the crowd, the buzzing, busy crowd. I need her to talk to Chera right now. I don't know what to say. "Listen, these things happen; it'll be all right." *Did I just say that?* I tell her that I had a friend who died in high school, not to make her feel better, but to let her know that I know the hurt. I tell her that I'll tell her mom. Even from miles away, her mother can wrap her arms around her and make her feel better. I'm talking while sitting on the edge of a table there in the Houston arena because my feet still hurt so badly from the running. The pain won't stop. Then I feel bad for thinking about my feet.

When we get home, we wrap our arms around Chera for real. She sobs like a little baby in her mother's arms, huge, wracking sobs that I haven't heard from her since she was a real baby. Only then the pain was usually in her toe or knee or head—usually because she'd just smashed into some furniture. Then I could rub the pain away. Now the ache is in her heart, and I can't touch it. I'm angry at death. I'm selfish, and I want to fix this, to help Chera understand how death works—like I would know. But for now I'm just angry.

A couple of days later, I wear my new shoes as I run to the top of Tiger Hill. I'm by myself because Chera's at school. On the way down I feel the sharp stab of pain in my heels once again. I'm barely able to hobble home. But once I get there, I give each shoe a good twisting, like the guy in the shoe store had done, thinking maybe they just aren't broken in right yet. The next day I go back up the hill, and I feel the pain starting up again. *Run through it,* I tell myself. *What?* Sometimes I'm not sure I'm hearing myself right. *Run through it,* I say again. You know, like Rudy at Notre Dame, Rocky in *Rocky I, II, III, IV,* and *V,* and that Christian guy who ran all the time in *Chariots of Fire*. Whenever they felt some incredible pain, they'd just "run through it." Even though that doesn't sound so medically smart, I run anyway. If I still hurt when I get back home, I decide, I'll have to tell Chera that the race is off. But if I can run through it…

I play the *Rocky* theme in my head. And I run, and I run, *and I run through it*! I surprise myself. When I get back to the house, the pain has stopped. For the first time in two weeks, neither of my heels hurt. Which is good, because there are only two weeks left to the race.

"Dad, are you ready to run to Tiger Hill?" Chera asks me. Finally, we're going to run together. We haven't been able to do that too much because of our schedules. The marathon is in only two days. We bought our running clothes the day before, and we want to try them out—to break them in and all. That will also give us a chance to check for chafing. The last thing I want is to run twenty-six-point-two miles and find out (probably after that first mile) that my shorts are dangerous.

So we stretch a bit in the front yard and then casually begin our lope. From the front yard we can see the fire tower at the top of Tiger Hill, where we're going. It looms out there like a mountain peak, never seeming to get any closer. My front porch is Depression Rock on Pikes Peak.

Today is a beautiful spring day—hot, almost. And we look sharp in our matching blue shorts and white tops. We look *athletic*.

At the base of Tiger Hill, about two miles from the house, where the hill noticeably begins to rise up from the flat ground, the asphalt changes color, becomes darker. Usually, I run to that spot and then walk to the top, but today we keep running. Today is different. We both sense it once we cross the line. I'm waiting for Chera to stop, to catch her breath. But that doesn't happen. We keep running. Leaning into the hill and breathing deeply.

"Let's try to get to that mailbox," I say, wanting to break this giant hill down into little parts. We're running in molasses. We're lifting our legs, our knees, pushing forward but barely moving.

"To that next drive," Chera grunts, once we've made it to the mailbox. And since we made it to the mailbox, I figure we must be moving.

"See where the color changes?" I ask, waving a limp hand ahead of us at a dark patch in the road. She understands what I'm asking, and we push on.

Once, when we've reached a spot where it appears we're just about to the top, we find lots more hill left. A false summit. We saw this at Pikes Peak. False summits are like false hope.

"Come on, Chera!" I call, remembering the day I'd tasted my own vomit on this same hill, only farther down. We're way past that point where I had wanted to die. We're pushing so hard, driving our legs ahead with such determination, that when we finally come to a level spot, we almost tip over face first.

"Yay! We did it!" I shout and try to do the Rocky dance, but my arms are like wet noodles. Chera's red and grinning, and her face shines with perspiration. She bends over, hands on her knees, trying to catch her breath. We take a moment to enjoy this moment, to look out over our small town spread out in the valley below while we drink some water that we brought along, before our long start downhill. And since the downhill is hard on the knees, we walk to the bottom, into the valley. As we walk we talk about death—sort of.

"I think about her every day," Chera says, between breaths.

I know she's talking about Elizabeth. It's been almost two weeks, and I'm thinking, *Of course you do.* But instead of saying that, instead of just acknowledging her pain and loss, I want to find a way to explain *why* she feels the way she feels. I'm supposed to know these things. I want to fix this. I've got an idea:

"When you're sixteen—" I don't like how this is going already. So I start over. "You don't get over death so quickly," I say. "I read a poem once about someone who grieved a death—it was right after your mom's sister, Cheralyn, died."

Cheralyn was fifteen, a freshman in high school, when Chonda and I were seniors. This was before I'd started dating Chonda, though Chonda and I had kissed once. Cheralyn was tall with long blond hair and was skinny as a stick. She was always talking about God to friends, to strangers, to people who sat next to her in school, to me. She had no way of knowing that I had lost him—that I was looking for him. Of course, I never told her this either.

Cheralyn grew ill one Friday night and after a few days was no better. So her mother took her to the doctor and they ran some tests, and before long the doctor came out and told them that Cheralyn had leukemia. The whole school was devastated. We rallied around Chonda and her family. We had fund-raisers, we sent cards and stuffed animals that filled up her room, and we went to the hospital in caravans just to visit Cheralyn. The fifth-floor lobby was always full of family and friends who sat around and discussed all the ways the doctors had of fixing this. But for all the talk, twenty-one days after we got the bad news, Cheralyn died. I was one of the pallbearers at the funeral. All the other pallbearers were high-school kids as well, friends of mine. Every week for over a year after the funeral, I'd visit the cemetery by myself. I made sure to tell Cheralyn how Chonda and I were doing, but mostly I'd sit in the grass and stare at the hump of earth that covered her body.

I had no skills for dealing with something like this.

So I stared at the grave, just staring at this rise I couldn't seem to get over.

Shortly after this, I found a poem. I've forgotten who wrote it or any of the words, but I remembered its essence. In this poem someone has lost someone near to him, someone he loved. The first year of grief was the worst—first Christmas, first birthday, first anniversary of the death. The second year was hard but not as bad, and every year after that got easier (for lack of a better word).

"You never forget," I tell Chera as we walk down the hill together, remembering the times I sat cross-legged on the young grass next to Cheralyn's grave. "But you don't hurt as badly—not like you're aching now." I shake my head. We're nearly to the bottom of Tiger Hill. "I didn't believe the poem at first, because I was still hurting so badly then. But it was right—the poem. Looking back now, I see it was right. Don't try to feel better now. Just hurt. Go ahead and miss her. Think about her all you want." It's hard to tell if she's listening to me. She's mulling something over in her head.

"I heard today," she says, "that when your neck is broken, you can live up to five minutes before you die."

"Yeah?"

"Maybe she thought about Jesus during that time."

I nod. "That's a good thought." And maybe because I'm thinking of Cheralyn, I think it sounds like something she would have said.

"Maybe she remembered something I said in class."

I nod again, but now I'm reflective. *People always remember the talks they have about God,* I think.

At the bottom of the hill the air is cooler, shaded, and it blows across us and feels refreshing. The hill is behind us now, and so we begin to run. I wish I could hurt for her, but it doesn't work that way. So we just run.

We don't go very far when we see a big man in the front yard of a simple house, planting azalea bushes. We wave and tell him how pretty his yard looks.

"How far did you make it?" he calls back to us, as he stands and brushes the loose dirt from his hands and points up Tiger Hill. He knows where we've come from.

"To the top!" I call back.

His eyes bug out and he shakes his head, as if he's been slugged by a boxer's mitt. He's funny. "To the *very* top?" he asks.

"To the *very* top," Chera says, borrowing his words. "We're getting ready for the marathon."

He waves us over. Another man, who's helping him plant the bushes, keeps on working. "The one to raise money for leukemia research?" he asks when we get close enough.

I remember that now from the brochure, so I nod.

The big man grins and says, "Then you're running for me." He pats his wide chest with both open hands. He steps closer to us, and we meet in his driveway with a handshake. "I'm Kevin Youse," he says. "Sounds like *mouse* but with a *Y.* Yes," he continues, "last year the doctors gave me four to six weeks to live." He raises his hands out to each side as if he were about to say, "Ta-da!" But instead he says, "I'm still here!"

"Praise God," Chera says.

"Yes," Kevin shoots back and points to Chera. "Praise God!"

While his buddy plants more bushes, Kevin tells us that it was probably the Agent Orange in Vietnam that caused his cancer. Chera and I nod like we're well aware of the Agent Orange problem. He says that over the years he's done lots of missions work in China, helped build churches all over the world. Now he's spreading the word in his neighborhood, enjoying spending time with his wife, fixing up the yard like he's always promised her he'd do, and riding his motorcycle.

"I got this while I was still taking chemo," he says, leading us to the huge motorcycle in his garage. "I always wanted a Harley." With a twist of a key and a push of a button, Kevin fires up the motorcycle, and it pops and growls and rings and shakes the whole garage until I think a few tools on the pegboard will shake right off.

He kills the engine and says, "That marathon is this week, ain't it?"

"Two days from now," says Chera.

"I thought so. I got a friend running too, and she's in a cool down now."

"A cool down?" I ask.

"Yeah. She told me you're not supposed to run the week before the race. Let the muscles build up."

I've never heard this before. "Oh yeah," I say. "Well, we're not doing much today. Just up the hill and down. It's only five and a half miles. Just a warmup during the cool down."

He nods as if that makes sense to him, or maybe he's just being polite. We finally say good-bye to Kevin and his motorcycle and jog on to the house. "Ever hear of a cool-down period?" I ask Chera as we run. She shakes her head. "I wonder how important a cool-down period is?" She shakes her head again.

The next day, the day before the race, I make sure our running clothes are clean and we have fresh socks, and when Chera comes home from school I say, "Let's go see Kevin." I think I have a good idea.

"Kevin Youse? That rhymes with 'mouse'?"

"Yeah."

"For what?"

"Let's ask him to pray for us."

Chera's face lights up, as if that's the best idea she's ever heard. Don't know what made me think to do this, but it seems it's something we *should* do. So we drive over and find Kevin and his friend still in the front yard, still planting azaleas (he tells us he's got about fifty of them) and some dogwood trees.

When we tell him we want him to pray for us, for the race, he comes up off his knees quickly, brushes away the dirt and grass, and puts one big arm around each of us so he can draw us in close. "Sure thing," he says. We huddle there in the yard while Kevin prays for us, for strength, endurance, perseverance, for our race. I close my eyes and hear somewhere behind me a shovel hitting rocks and loose dirt.

He prays for about two minutes, doling out strength to each of us. When he finishes, he glances at his watch and says, "Oh my goodness. I've got to go get more mulch before they close. Good luck, guys."

We thank him and leave. As I'm driving away, I look in the rearview mirror, and I can see the long, narrow strip of road that leads to the summit of Tiger Hill. And I see Kevin Youse's house, the front yard spotted with dozens of freshly planted azaleas that haven't bloomed yet. For the first time I notice that the road dips just a bit right there at the foot of the hill, right there in front of Kevin's house. The road dips, and the asphalt changes color, gets darker, as it starts to swell. Kevin lives in the valley at the foot of Tiger Hill. A real valley, and a real shadow of death.

Why does one man survive a disease that's supposed to have killed him in six weeks while a sixteen-year-old girl slides off the shoulder of the road and dies in her car in a few short minutes? I can't think of a poem—any poem—that will help me understand this. It's true: sometimes we aren't meant to understand certain things.

A marathon race is an experience something like that of a festival, a circus, an athletic event, and Southern brunch all rolled into one.

The race officially starts at 7:30 a.m. But we have to be there at 6:00. (It's in the participant's manual.) We've already registered and are wearing our bib numbers and have fastened these little computer chips to our shoe-strings so the race people can keep track of our times. The weather is chilly (for shorts and tank top), about sixty, and the sun hasn't come up yet. Over nine thousand racers pace about and stretch in the hazy twilight on the grassy lawn of Centennial Park in downtown Nashville. There are lots of free bananas, so we take some.

"Are bananas good for runners?" I ask Chera.

She doesn't know, but she has to shrug to answer me because she's eating a banana.

When we're ready to stretch, she teaches me a few of the stretches she's learned from high-school track, and so we do these until we're sick of stretching, but we still have an hour before the big race starts. That's when I start making up stretches, like the Lean Back. This is where I stand straight and lean back until I almost fall over. And every time—when I almost fall over—I have to stumble backward across the grass. I look silly and it makes Chera laugh. And then there's the one I do that looks more like a hip-hop step than an exercise. My hair is short, close-cropped, but I can feel it flopping against my scalp.

"What are you doing?" Chera asks me.

"How much longer?" I ask her, while I keep doing the Hippity-Hoppity Hip stretch that I just made up.

"Did Mom tell you Patrick and I are going out this weekend?"

I almost fall over. "Patrick? Whatever happened to this Brad-guy?" That's what I always call the boys she likes: (Name)-guy.

She shakes her head and stretches her calf. "He's just a friend. Besides, I think he's too old for me to date."

Oh. Of course. "And this Patrick-guy is?"

"You know. From church. And he works at New Frontiers. Larry and Lori like him."

I remember now. Patrick. "How old is he?"

"Sixteen. Just like me."

"Okay." I stretch some more. Normal stretches now because this is serious. "So what's this Patrick-guy do for a living?"

"Daaaaaad."

We're wearing our Yale sweatshirts, souvenirs I'd gotten a couple of months earlier when I'd gone to Connecticut. I guess there in the predawn mist, eating bananas and doing complicated stretches, we must look like a couple of Ivy Leaguers. At least one fellow thinks so. "So you guys go to Yale?" a man asks. He's my height, skinny, and sporting a full beard. He's standing there next to us, trying to pull one foot as far behind him as possible without tipping over. I shake his hand, but this doesn't stop him from pulling on his foot.

"No," I answer. "We just have the shirts."

He seems at a loss as to what to say next, as if he'd never talked to someone who wasn't an Ivy Leaguer but who had the shirts. "Oh," he says, startled. "I thought maybe you went to Yale."

"So where are you from?" Chera asks him. She's much friendlier than I am. I'm ready for another banana.

"Chicago," he says. He switches feet and grimaces as he gives the other one a good tug.

"Run many marathons?" I ask him.

"A few. How about you?"

We shake our heads and grin, and confess that this is our first. He seems to grow taller, to swell with self-importance. "So have you run twenty-six miles before?" he asks from above.

"I've run ten," I say, and leave out the part about hurting arches and my new shoes and all.

"And I've run seven and a half," Chera says.

He looks at us both, and there, in the last of the twilight haze, I'm sure he smirks. And I don't think it has anything to do with tugging on his feet or the bananas. Now, with both feet back on the ground, he tells us, "Well, you *might* make it."

"We're going to try," I tell him, kind of leaning in close to him to say it, as if he's hard of hearing. Then Chera and I take our bananas and go to stretch somewhere else.

When the time is right, all nine thousand of us are herded from the park to the main street where the starting line is. We're in corral number nine. There are only ten. From where we are, we can't see Amy Grant singing the national anthem or Vince Gill firing the starting gun. But when the anthem ends, we hear the cheers and then we hear a big *bang*! Vince has fired. Chera and I take off, like foxes let loose from a box—only after a couple of strides we stop abruptly and nearly knock down the man in front of us.

"Sorry," I say.

I look at Chera and she says, "Don't look at *me*." There's nowhere to go. We're walled in on all sides by people in tank tops. We creep, with everyone else, to the starting line, and not until we cross the rubber mat— the real starting line—does the avenue open up and we begin to run.

Lots of people have planned to walk the whole way (why they were in corral numbers higher than us, I don't know). But we have to run past them, dodging to the right and left, saying "Excuse me" a jillion times.

Along this first mile people litter the street with dozens of sweatshirts, peeling out of them because of the quick warmup. We're going up a small slope now, and the street rolls down behind us, and when I glance back it looks like a tornado has blown through a yard sale.

We drop into our familiar "let's run to Tiger Hill" pace. Pass some while others pass us. A different country music band plays at every mile, usually one no one's ever heard of, but I know the songs. At mile three the band is loud and everyone seems happy and they're clapping and they want to know why old Hank still drinks. Chera's never heard the song, so while still singing and clapping and jogging, I try to explain it to her. "You see, back long ago, old Hank's daddy, Hank Sr.—" But when I hear that still, small voice in my head—*Yeah, you* might *make it*—I decide to conserve my energy and just run. It's not like Chera's dying for a country music lesson anyway.

I carry my cell phone in my belly pouch because Chonda is out of town and wants to call us sometime during the race. She calls from Spokane, Washington, when we're at the four-mile marker, sounding surprised to learn that we've run four miles without a single problem. She's on her way home but will have to change planes in Minneapolis, so she promises to call then, just to make sure we're still okay.

At every mile, tables are filled with water cups and a grape power drink. This is the part I've seen Frank Shorter do on television, so I lead the way to show Chera how it's done. I grab the first cup from one of the volunteers, who's holding her arm fully extended. I spill part of the grape drink, but that's okay. Without slowing I tip the cup back, and half of the juice goes up my nose, and I nearly drown. Chera sees what's happened to me and stops to drink hers. So we lose a few steps to take a drink, but if we have to stop for CPR, we could be completely out of the race. I'll do better next time.

The race is a festival. At every turn there's something to marvel at, or moan at, or at least to raise your eyebrows about. There are four Dolly Partons, all running together, wearing short skirts, cowgirl boots, vests with fringe around the edges, and other Dolly Parton accessories—like big hair. They pass us once, and then we pass them when they stop to have their picture taken with some spectators. I can't figure out if they're women dressed like Dolly or men dressed like Dolly. Either way, they're pretty and surprisingly athletic.

One man runs while playing a guitar. We see him at about the five-mile marker and again later. He talks with people around him and then tries to write a song using their name. Right there on the spot. "What's your name, darlin'? Chera? Let's see, *Oh there is a girl named Chera who runs just like a deera...*" After sixteen miles of running and strumming, he's very tired.

The men at a rescue mission, men with shoes and without, with teeth and without, some needing shaves and all needing showers, are standing there on the sidewalk and clapping for us. "Keep going," one man calls, his teeth snaggled and yellowed. "You guys are doing great!" I want to tell him the exact same thing, that he's doing great.

We've been running for eighteen miles, amazing ourselves since the ten-mile marker. I want to find Mr. Stretchy Man from Chicago and tell him how far we've already run and that we *are* going to make it, when we see an old, gray-haired black man wearing a T-shirt that reads I Love Jesus. He's clapping hard for us (even though there are about five thousand other racers ahead of us—Mr. Stretchy Man probably one of them).

"I like your shirt!" Chera calls. The man claps harder and smiles and waves us on with his arms. The breeze he creates that gently pushes at our backs, this is his gift.

A woman gives us Snickers bars at mile nineteen and saves our lives. We run right by the big church where I prayed and praised while I was in college. It's also where Chera went as a little girl. She barely remembers it.

It's during the second half of the race that we sometimes stop running and instead try to walk real fast, power walk, or sometimes power limp. The calves and hamstrings are sore and stiff and cramp. We stop to stretch a lot, but the hurt won't go away, so we keep running. When we hit the twenty-four-mile marker, a brusque woman with a raspy voice tells us that we only have two more miles to go before we can get a beer. That doesn't exactly inspire us, but several other people do pass us on that turn.

With two miles to go I tell Chera, "Let's run all the way in. No stopping, no walking."

"Serious?"

"Serious."

"Because of the beer?"

"Come on! It's just like Tiger Hill," I say. I hop and skip and try to shake out all the pain from my legs and back. (I'm beginning to think the new hip-hop stretch thing I was doing at the beginning has done some good.) "Come on! To the finish line!" I say. "Only two miles!" And so we run anew.

The last two miles of this race is a pretty stretch through Shelby Park, mostly downhill as the road leads into a valley, into the lowland at the edge of a river. Once we reach the river, we'll follow it for over a mile to the coliseum where the Tennessee Titans play football. By now it seems most people are walking—but not us. We're keeping a pretty good pace now. And the more people we pass, the faster we try to go.

"How do you feel?" I ask Chera.

She nods, wets her lips. "I'm okay," she says. Just then the phone rings. I dig it out of my belly pouch. It's Chonda.

"Only two miles to go," I tell her.

"You're kidding!"

Why would I be kidding?

"No way," I say. "We're going to make it. We'll call you at the finish line."

For us, it's as if the race is just beginning. All this time, up hills, down hills, around turns we couldn't see beyond, past bands we really couldn't hear, with promises of beer and reminders of a loving God, these were all preludes to these last two miles. Along the river we run, patches of water visible through young green leaves of spring. A man is clapping and encouraging us onward, saying, "You're almost there. Around the corner you'll see the marker."

And he's right. We turn a corner, now weaving through and around people like we were at the beginning, finding new wind and new strength. There, like all the other markers, is the big placard that reads 26. Only point-two miles beyond that is the finish line. We can see people, lots of people, grouped up just ahead. As we get closer we see that they're forming a lane and that the route leads through this lane. But we still can't see the finish line. Not until we turn that final corner and find ourselves surrounded by hundreds of people on each side do we see it: the finish line. It looks just like the starting line, and for an instant, I feel as if we've gone on this incredible journey of people (four Dolly Partons) and places (my old college church) only to wind up where we started. Lots of runners are crossing the finish line ahead of us, and rising up from both sides of the lane is a continuous cheer for those who've run the race and fought the fight and are about to finish.

This is us racing into heaven. Chera and I begin to sprint. It only seems right to run at full speed across the line, since this is a race. We fly past other runners, embarrassing them, I'm sure. I imagine they envy our energy. I feel the breeze created by our speed blowing against my face. The spectators to the right and left blur. Instead of people cheering, I see Kevin Youse on his Harley; I see Elizabeth Jones sitting in English class next to Chera; I see Cheralyn and she's smiling because Chonda and I got married; I see the guy who sold me the sneakers; I see the road that leads up to Tiger Hill; and I see my dad sitting cross-legged on a kitchen chair, leaning toward the images of the summer Olympics on a snowy television set. Just before we cross the padded starting line, I reach over and take Chera's hand. She clasps mine and grins at me.

Electronic *beep.*

We finish at 5:35:04. And even though that's good enough to capture 4,474th and 4,475th place, the "We're number one!" chant goes off in my head and won't stop.

Shortly after we cross the finish line, someone drapes Mylar blankets over each of us, but in spite of the tinfoil, we still manage to hug. Now we take the victory walk. Before us are rows and rows of all sorts of fruits, drinks, and snacks. It really is heaven. And Elvis is there too. We pass on having our pictures taken with him and instead head for the snacks.

The medal ceremony is not really a ceremony at all. Several people are taking one medal at a time from big boxes filled with thousands of medals. They place them around the necks of runners as fast as they come in. We present our necks and a hurried woman slips them over our heads and rushes us on by. When I get the chance, I lift mine from my chest and see that there are words and designs stamped on it that all mean something, I'm sure. But more than the decorations, I love the heaviness of it—in my hand, against my chest. This is not a toy. This will not be in a future yard sale. Chera squeezes hers tightly, appreciating the spoils of a hard-fought victory, and tries to read it upside down. She's talked about this medal for days and days, and now it's hers—all hers. And even though there are nine thousand other people with medals just like it, what each represents is unique: the separate sacrifices, the separate pains, and the moments of perseverance— most likely multiplied by thousands and thousands. Maybe there are nine thousand medals just alike. But there are nine thousand different stories here too, and today each one ends here at the same place: the finish line. Heaven.

And that's the end of the race for us. The walk from the finish line to the parking lot is probably the toughest, much tougher to do than the last two miles of the race. For now the adrenaline is gone and the aches are great—the greatest yet. We go home and shower and then go pick up Chonda at the airport. She's been traveling all day and is tired. Yet when she sees us, she smiles. Of course, she's able to recognize us by the shiny, bronze-colored medals we wear about our necks.

4

Twice to Heaven

We celebrate at the top
of Blanca Peak—14,345 feet.

I find a newspaper story about a man who lives down the street from us who recently tried to climb Mount Rainier in Washington but didn't make it to the top because of the weather. "I'm going back," my neighbor says in the article. "I love a challenge." There were other things in this article as well, like the mention of blowing snow, glaciers that suddenly split open to create bottomless pits, and a moving description of a man who comes to complete exhaustion but never even makes it to the top.

I just finish reading the story for the third time when I approach Chera and say, "How about we climb Mount Rainier?" Her face lights up, and that whole *vicarious* thing goes right out the window.

"Sure. Where is it?"

So I tell her what I know about the snow-capped mountain in Washington, mostly from what I've just read in the newspaper article. But I've also read this Marianne Moore poem once (no kidding) about the "frozen octopus" known as Mount Rainier. I'll dig through my old school books and find it again.

"So I could use my crampons?" (She'd gotten a pair of the spiked shoes for Christmas that year—just in case something like this would happen.)

"Yep. And a rope, and an ice ax, and some mittens."

She pumps her fists into the air and screams, "Yes! Really? An ice ax like I've seen on TV?" She's right: all mountain climbers on television have ice axes. Sometimes it's the weapon the bad guy uses to kill the good guy (who's usually the reluctant guide) so he (the bad guy) can have all the money for himself. That kind of ice ax. Very dangerous.

We check Web sites and read survival stories about the 14,408-foot peak of Mount Rainier.

"Do you know Mount Rainier is an inactive volcano, just like Mount St. Helens?" I ask Chera.

"What's Mount St. Helens?"

I raise my eyebrows, trying not to convey too much surprise that she hasn't heard of it, and say, "An inactive volcano that blew its top in 1980."

"Cool," she says.

Mount St. Helens: "Cool." You'd think I'd given her a present.

"Did you know," she tells me one day, snapping a single sheet of paper in one hand that she reads from, "that eighty-three people have died on Mount Rainier?"

"I didn't know that." Concern.

"Yeah, mostly in the winter, though."

"We're going in August," I tell her.

She nods. "Oh yeah. Should be very safe that time of the year."

We continue to lay out these dangers for each other, with as much detail inserted (or deleted) as suits the purpose, as if they're appetizers on a platter. It's just a little game we play. "I read the other day," Chera tells me out of the blue, "that it can be sunny and clear in Seattle, but a blizzard can kick up and cover the whole mountain in seconds"—dramatic pause— "and anyone who happens to be on it." Ominous music plays in my head.

I recover, and the next day I say to her, "Larry and Lori told me they know someone who fell on his ice ax and stabbed himself in the heart"— pause—"died instantly." Now we both hear the music and sit in silence and think about what we're saying and what we're thinking of doing.

But we remind ourselves that we're going with a guide service. We'll be with professionals the whole time. They won't let that sort of stuff (stab- bings, avalanches, volcanic eruptions) happen to us. So we make all the plans to climb Mount Rainier. The challenge is set for August 1, 2000.

Chera calls me from camp one day with an incredible plan. "Larry and Lori are taking a group of teens to Colorado for two weeks, and they want me to go with them."

"That sounds great," I tell her. That would be July 1, a month before we go to Mount Rainer.

"And guess what."

"What?"

"We're going to climb *two* mountains."

"No way!"

"Can you come?"

Can we do the TV show? Can we do the TV show? Can we? Let's talk to the man who lives at the top of the volcano!

I'm thinking.

Chera tells me they'll be taking the teenagers (troubled teens, she says) out in a couple of vans.

"I could meet you on the trail," I say. It's more like a question.

"You can do that?"

"Sure?" I mean, "Sure." *I hope I can, anyway.* "Let me talk to Larry and Lori and I'll get directions."

"Which one?"

"Which what?"

"Larry *or* Lori?"

"Oh yeah, Larry." I never think of them separately.

I cash in some frequent flyer miles and a week later catch a plane to Colorado Springs *(Hello, Pikes Peak!)*, rent a car, and then start driving south to the trailhead. That's where I'm supposed to meet them—on the trailhead of Blanca Peak, the fourth tallest mountain in Colorado at 14,345 feet. That's the plan I'd made with Larry on the telephone that night. We were looking at maps, and I was trying to find the red and blue squiggly lines he was talking about.

"Okay," I said, "Is it a fat red line or a skinny red line?"

"It's a skinny red line, but it crosses over a fat blue one. See that one?"

"No, wait. I see a skinny red, but it crosses over a skinny blue one."

"No, not it."

"Is your skinny blue one just as skinny as the red one, or is it just a skosh fatter?"

He paused for time to measure. "They look the same to me. I think I see the fat blue one you're talking about. The one I'm talking about is up about an inch from there."

So the direction giving went well. Only now I'm out here on the highway, and nothing is color coded.

From Colorado Springs to the trailhead is a three-hour drive, so it's nearly six o'clock by the time I find the vans. I missed the skinny squiggly line twice before finally seeing two tiny white specks at the base of this great span of peaks. Behind me is all flat. This is the end of the Sangre de Cristo mountain range, and Blanca Peak is the tallest mountain until you get down to Mexico somewhere.

I park beside the vans, and just the sight of the long U-Haul trailer with Tennessee plates has my heart pounding. I'm excited in a Lewis and Clark kind of way: I've crossed the entire country in search of something I've only heard about (that night on the phone with Larry and Lori—or just Larry, rather). I can't wait to slip up behind Chera and say something like, "You guys mind if I join you?" That will be so clever. That's what I'm thinking. But I'll have to hurry, because I figure I only have about two and a half hours of daylight left. Larry told me it's about a five-mile hike up to Lake Como, where they'll set up camp. Simple.

Everything I brought from Nashville is in my backpack, so I wrestle it from the trunk, strap it on—about forty-five pounds—and head right up the trail. I'm in a hurry. For fun I've brought my GPS this time and check myself at seventy-eight hundred feet. *Wow,* I think. *Only five hours earlier I was at seven hundred feet!*

I probably go a hundred yards when I have to stop and sit down. *Too fast. Slow down. After all, only five hours earlier I was at seven hundred feet.*

All the pains, and memories of pains, of Pikes Peak come rushing back, starting in my lower back, with an unbelievable pressure that mashes my kidneys. I decide it's the kind of pain that can only come by standing on a steep incline with at least forty pounds parked on those last two vertebrae just above the tailbone.

The trail is straight and steep without a single switchback, like Tiger Hill back home, only longer. Every time I stop I look back to see that the vans and my rental car have shrunk a bit more. I can't get over how different this trail is from Pikes Peak—*less commercial,* I'm thinking, *and more— what's the word?—wild.* On Pikes Peak the trail is packed and hard, and some places are as smooth as concrete. This trail is landscaped with round stones, like those round ornamental stones you can buy at Home Depot for your water garden, and every one is loose and wobbly. And because of this I can never plant a solid step. I can only pick up my boot in the middle of a wobble and quickly try the next one. I almost fall. *Ah! I almost fell!* I steady myself by bending my knees and tilting from front to back and back to front. I reach out to both sides, the same kind of motion a man high-wire walking would make. *This is not mountain climbing,* I think. *This is surfing.*

And it's so hot. It's in the upper eighties. I drink lots of water, and when I take a sit-down break after about an hour and take off my pack, I discover that all the water I've drunk has leaked out my back. I reach back and squeeze my shirt, and sweat drips off my fingers. My GPS tells me I've gained about eight hundred feet in elevation. The lake is at twelve thousand feet, so I figure I have more than four hours to go, which isn't good because there's only an hour or so of daylight left.

Not long ago I learned a trick whereby I can tell almost to the minute when the sun will set. First, you hold your hand up so that your little finger lies along the horizon. Then count how many fingers between the sun and the horizon. Each finger is about fifteen minutes (unless you have really skinny fingers). So with about three and a half hours of hiking to go to reach the lake, I only have about one and a half hours of sun left. I'm glad I packed a flashlight.

There are no big trees on this part of the trail, no forest like on the first part of Pikes Peak. It's desert-like, dry and scrubby, with lots of short, gnarled bushes. When I stop for air and water, I hunker down next to a squatty bush that only comes up to my chin. It's small shade, but it works—so long as I don't stand up.

And then I realize I'm lost. Larry had told me to stay to the right when I get to a fork in the trail. But it hadn't looked like a fork. I saw a rough place here; I saw a rough place there. *That* was the fork. The trail starts going downhill, and I'm losing altitude. *No, no! This can't be right.* Lake Como is at twelve thousand feet. Larry and Lori are at twelve thousand feet. Two vans of teenagers are at twelve thousand feet. Chera is at twelve thousand feet. The sun is barely above the horizon now—three fingers. I can't be going down! I double back and it takes me twenty minutes to get back to that rough spot on the trail, which is the fork. So I've lost forty minutes. I drink more water.

I'm back on the main trail now, and I can see dozens of different boot tracks. One pattern is clear—most likely made by the end hiker, not necessarily the slowest, but perhaps the most responsible, pulling up the rear, checking over her shoulder to see if I'm catching up. Incongruously, there's a fresh lollipop stick. I don't pick it up and sniff, but I wonder what a professional tracker would make of that. Still, this reassures me.

The trail never gets easier. Every step is a dance. And now, after knowing that I *could* make a wrong turn, I'm worried that I could get lost again.

That's when I see the first solid sign, a real sign and not just a lollipop stick. In the middle of the trail, weighted with a nice smooth garden stone to keep it from blowing away, is a handwritten note that reads *Water for David,* and there's an arrow below the message that points to the right. It's signed *Chera.* I laugh aloud, and a surprising husky sound comes out of my throat. This altitude and dust is affecting everything.

I pick up the note, read it over and over, trace my fingers over the bumpy surface that mirrors the stones that had rested beneath it because someone (Chera) had smoothed it out flat on the uneven ground so I'd be sure to see it.

I walk on with renewed strength and figure I must be "real close." I'm so excited, in fact, I don't even take the time to get the water from the stream my daughter has so painstakingly marked for me.

Only one more finger of sunlight to go, about fifteen more minutes. Where are they? I'm barely over ten thousand feet now, after a good two and a half hours on the trail (forty minutes of that going in the wrong direction), and still a long way from the lake. Something is stirring up ahead, on the trail. A lone hiker is making his way down. He's toting a much smaller pack than mine and sporting the beginnings of a beard.

"Are you David?" he asks me, as if he recognizes me.

"Yes, I am," I answer, rather dryly, amazed to hear my name called by a strange man in a strange place.

He jerks a thumb back over his shoulder as he passes on by. "Well, a big group is waiting up there for you. About a mile ahead."

"At Lake Como?"

"Nah. They didn't make it to the lake."

"About a mile?"

"Yep."

"Thanks."

I keep on walking, but I'm having difficulty breathing. It's the altitude and the dust and the terrible way the combination is affecting my sinuses. So there, at over ten thousand feet, I do something that I've never done before—swore I would never do—but have seen my father do countless times. I take the forefinger of my right hand and place it firmly against my nose, mashing in the right nostril. Then I tilt my head, until my nose is aimed at the valley far, far below me (I figure there's plenty of room there), and blow. The feeling and the sound sicken me, but the results are heavenly. I stand, and just like my father always did, I smile—because now I can breathe. *I hope I never have to do that again,* I say to myself. And I don't think I'll ever do that again—right after I take care of the right nostril.

I move on and the sun moves down, and finally, in the twilight, I stop to dig out my flashlight. The dark has caught me. No need to hurry now. I know they can't be too far ahead of me. I have a flashlight and two brand-new double-A batteries. I'll be fine. Before moving on, I sit and soak in the sight of the dimming valley below me. I sit here, able to see for hundreds of miles across the flat plains of southern Colorado. Gilded grasses. Spots of light from houses and barns far, far away could be lightning bugs that won't blink off. I drink the last of my water and soak in everything else through my eyeballs. *Right now,* I think, *not another living soul knows where I am.* And although I'm totally isolated, I'm so full of wonder that it's impossible to feel alone.

The sun is gone. No more fingers above the horizon. So I follow the trail in the disappearing twilight. The whitish rocks seem to glow. They've stored daylight like bricks will store the sun's heat, and now radiate into the night. (Or maybe they're just reflecting the stars' glow.)

I have my flashlight handy and ready. But I only use it twice—once to make sure the batteries are working, and a second time to illuminate a stump shaped like a bear.

I hear the chatter and giggling of teenage voices. Then I see the lights bouncing around in the darkness.

"Hey, David," I hear. I still don't turn my light on. It's Larry—I can tell from the glow of the rocks—and he greets me as if I've been by his side all day and had just stepped away for a moment. He must have been pretty confident of his directions. "There's some food up ahead. Get all you want." And then he goes about his business of setting up camp.

"David, is that you?" It's Lori who asks. She's sitting in the middle of a semicircle of some twenty-four teenagers who are all splayed about—cross-legged, on stomachs, on backs, on sides, balled up in fetal positions. Teenagers are everywhere. Only I don't see Chera. "There's plenty of food right over there," she says and points to a big pot that looks like a stump, which looks like a bear, in the dim light. "Help yourself."

Everyone, even though I don't know them yet, waves and welcomes me. I tell all the dark forms and shapes that it's good to see them all. I still don't see Chera. I slip my pack to the ground, and all the water that has leaked out my back has soaked my shirt and is starting to freeze, so I dig out a fresh shirt, a big sweatshirt. Lori hands me a pan of some kind of noodles, and even though I'm so hungry, they still taste awful, so I don't finish. There's a young lady standing close by wearing a Yale sweatshirt and a Petzl lamp on her head, but it's not on. "So did you have any trouble?" this girl asks, one of the troubled teens, I guess.

"Not much," I answer, working on the noodles, looking off into the dark shapes. "Yale University," I say, pointing to her shirt. "I've got one almost like that. I went there this year and picked one up as a souvenir—"

I start to say *I got one for my daughter and me* when suddenly I realize she *is* my daughter—wearing the shirt I'd bought for her! It's Chera standing before me! But it *is* dark, and she *is* wearing that contraption on her head, and she has a new haircut, and I haven't seen her in a couple of weeks, and she seems so much older—but mostly it's dark.

"So, Chera," I start my next sentence without letting her know I hadn't recognized her. I can't hug her now, because she'll know. And if I don't hug her at all, it'll seem as if I haven't even missed her, that I just zipped up the trail without wondering where she was and if she was safe. And if I don't hug her she won't know how I had really, really appreciated that note back there and would have gone crazy and jumped off the mountain had I not found it when I had. *Man, now what do I do? I'll give her a hug anyway and tell her how silly I am.* That's what I'm thinking, as I stab the cold noodles with my spoon *(clank, clank)* and take a bite *(yuck!)* and say in-stead, "So, Chera, how in the world are you doing?"

That first night we sleep on the trail or anywhere off to either side, any place we can find a level spot. Boys on one side, girls on the other. We don't build a fire because it's too dry and too dangerous. After tossing my noodles into the weeds, I find out that I'm tenting with a young man named Patrick. *Patrick? Patrick? Is this the same Patrick Chera told her mother and me about?* "Hi, Mr. Pierce," I hear someone say. In the glow of a lantern, I see a young man I recognize. It's Patrick. I remember meeting him before. He seemed like a nice guy then. But now he's the enemy, and I have to share a two-man tent with him.

"Hello, Patrick." I wonder if that was too steely.

He's grinning. Even in the dark I can see that. "I've already set the tent up," he says. "We're just over there." He points into the dark, but I can't see that far.

"I'll just follow you," I say.

"Good night, Dad," Chera calls as Patrick leads me off the trail, into the night.

"Good night."

"Good night, Patrick."

"Good night."

This feels weird.

I can't sleep here next to Patrick. So I lie still on my back and listen to him sleep. I can't sleep, and it's all his fault: he set the tent up on a slope. Now, I'm afraid that if I nod off I'll roll over on him. Besides, it's cold, and I can't breathe through my nose, and I'm still hungry because the noodles just hadn't done it for me, and my back hurts. This is not a good night.

At the first signs of light, I crawl out of the tent, way before anyone else, and sit stiffly in the early morning haze with my back against a giant gray rock. Somewhere close by I hear a stream. Otherwise, all is quiet and still and damp. In the first light I can see a patch of color here and there, a peak, a dome, peeping up through pine branches or scrubby low greenery. It's the sprawl of tents along both sides of the trail. It looks as if a tent truck had a wreck here. I can see now that we've chosen a site where there's no soft grass, not even dirt. We've all slept on stone. I wonder if everyone is going to feel as lousy as I do.

And there's such a big climb ahead.

Stretched out before me is that same valley I'd watched disappear a few hours earlier at dusk, only now the gilding is on the opposite side of the grass blades—the morning side, the eastern side.

I'm not alone for long. Up the trail trudges a young man dressed in well-worn loose jeans and a baggy sweatshirt. A pair of sandals protect his feet, and he leans into his walking stick with every other step.

"Good morning," I say when he's close enough.

"Hi."

He's a teenager and has a pleasant face. *Must have slept soundly,* I think. He stops before me, but I keep my seat. "My name's David," I continue.

"I'm…I'm…I'm…," and he stutters so badly that he can't get his name out. I'm beginning to be embarrassed for him, so I interrupt and say, "So, what's the plan for today?" I figure he must be keen to get to the next step of this adventure.

"I was going down to…to…to fill my water bottle," the young man (whatever his name is) says.

I turn an ear in the direction I hear the running stream. "It sounds close," I say.

"I'll show you," he says. With more work than I let on, I manage to stand and follow him off the trail, down a steep grade to a flat span where the grass is waist high. Why hadn't we camped here? We're real close to the stream now. "That's weird," he says, stopping a few steps from the stream.

"What's that?" I ask, looking past him to see what could be so weird.

"This," and the boy turns to show me something glistening in his hand. It looks like fish eggs, clear and gelatinous, spread on his open palm, but we're too far from the stream still—maybe frog eggs. Frogs are amphibious. I figure he must have scraped them from a plant or some rocks there on the side of the trail.

"Where'd it come from?" I ask, leaning in for a closer look.

"My nose."

Oh. I didn't see that one coming. I straighten up and move quickly past my new friend, on toward the stream. "Hey," I call back over a shoulder, hoping to explain the stuff (fish eggs) in his hand, "altitude does strange stuff to a body." I look back to make sure he's following and see him sling his shiny hand out over the weeds.

At the streamside we fill our bottles (me handling my own bottle, of course), and when we get back to camp, more people are stirring. Eventually I meet everyone and find out that the young man I've walked to the stream with is named Alvin. In addition to the twenty-four teens—including Chera, Patrick, and Alvin—there are two adult counselors, who are husband and wife, and Larry and Lori, who are also husband and wife (and adults). With twenty-nine people packing up and eating and relieving themselves in the woods and brushing teeth and breaking camp and filling water bottles (stay on the trail, I advise as many as I can, or you'll get slimed), it's nearly ten before we begin to climb. Our goal that day is to make it to Lake Como at twelve thousand feet. We only have about two miles to go, about two thousand feet in altitude to gain, but every step will be a wobbly one. Only we can't take off until someone owns up to the wet noodles Larry found in the weeds. I hesitate. This is my first day on the trail, and I'm not sure how things work out here. Maybe someone else had felt the same way about them—only no one else speaks up. So I confess (by raising my hand) and clean and bag the garbage. Chera helps by holding the bag. I hope I haven't embarrassed her. I'm sorry about that. Mostly I'm sorry for what mountain noodles look like after a long night in the open air—sort of like fish eggs.

Chera isn't out here just for fun, like I am. She's a junior counselor, here to work. This is strange to me, watching Chera work while I just stand to the side and wait. She goes from camper to camper, checking backpacks, reminding someone about cleanup duty, others of water duty (filling bottles), others to just tie their shoelaces. She asks me how I slept, and I give her a thumbs-up. I think she wants me to say something about Patrick, but I don't.

One girl named Rose is a handful, and it looks like Chera could use some help. According to Rose, she's done everything and been everywhere: the captain of the basketball team, an expert horse rider, in homes on the East and West coasts, in the circus for a bit—and she's only thirteen!

We're hiking (surfing) up the trail when Chera tells me, in a hushed voice, "Rose has a severe self-esteem problem."

"You learned this at camp?"

"That, and how to properly poop in the woods," she says with a big grin.

I don't think it's so funny. I didn't know there was a *wrong* way.

Together we try to "encourage" Rose, who also happens to be an incredible whiner. Her pack is light, almost empty, and she sips water constantly, which means she has to stop, constantly, and usually sit. If Chera coddled her at all, it was before I got there. No coddling today.

"Get up and walk," Chera says, almost Scripture-like. Then she cinches her pack tighter and heads out at a pace that's hard for even me to keep up with. Rose whines. Chera keeps going. Rose follows.

"Can I walk with you?" Rose whines.

Without looking back Chera calls, "If you can keep up." She's a machine!

It's hard to imagine that you can climb so high up on such a steep mountain and then come to a flat spot big enough to hold a lake. We crest the last rise—Chera pulling Rose while I push her—to the jubilant screams and shouts of the beat-up and banged-up teenagers ahead of us. We're at our resting spot for the night.

Lake Como levels out the mountain for at least five acres. It's ice cold and placid, except for where trout rise to dimple the glassy surface. Lake Como is a deep breath on this breathless mountain. We hike to the far side of the lake and shed our heavy packs. Tents go up fast, and soon I see feet, some naked and some covered with nasty socks, protruding from all different shapes (round, rectangular, square, igloo) of tents. Neither Patrick nor myself decide to take an afternoon nap. I brought along a fishing pole, so I hike to the water's edge and drop a hook on to the still surface and watch it sink.

I pulled the hook loaded with worm back and forth through the black water along the bank. I was thirteen and I always caught fish like this, in this very spot at Big Bluff Creek. But Dad and I weren't having any luck that day, not for the whole weekend even, and this was the big weekend we'd been looking forward to, because this was the weekend of the big fishing rodeo. We didn't have a boat, so we fished from the bank, using worms and doughballs made of cornflakes and bananas. About all you could catch with this kind of bait were bluegills, catfish, and carp—big ones, we hoped.

The rodeo started on a Friday morning and ended late the next day, and there were lots of prizes for different fish categories, with a separate category for kids. Dad and I considered ourselves a couple of the best bank fishermen around, so we had all the confidence that we were going to win. I was going to catch a monster on my moving worm, and if Dad could only catch a bluegill as big as the one he'd caught the week before, the one he'd brought home and put in the spring back at the house, there was no doubt we'd win. But it just wasn't a good weekend for fishing. As it got closer to the deadline to turn in all catches, Dad pulled in a big carp, while I kept working the banks with no luck. It wasn't the biggest fish he'd ever caught, but I'd have been happy with it. We were about to give it up, to call it quits, to load up the truck and go back to the house, when suddenly Dad had a plan—a really good plan.

The next morning I crawl (this is the *only* way I can move at first) from our tent along with the rest of the group, and eat breakfast, which consists of Pop-Tarts and water that we've stolen from the trout and treated with iodine tablets. Rose is up too, sleepy and swollen, hair tangled, and socks black with mountain dirt and flopping over her toes. For some in our group, Lake Como is the summit. This is as far as they'll go. They won't be pushed any higher. But Rose decides to go because Chera is going.

Surprisingly, the first hour of the hike is not too strenuous. We're only carrying food and rain gear. We pass by two more lakes—Blue Lakes and Crater Lake. Crater Lake is where we lose a few more. The climb is getting tough again, and five teenagers decide to stay put. "We'll be back in a few hours," we tell them. And so we leave the five with one of the adults. Whenever we stop to look back, we can see them. Someone is always throwing rocks into the water. But mostly they're lying down, resting, breathing hard.

Crater Lake is also where Chera goes down. She's hurt her ankle and may not be able to go on. It's been hurting her for a while, but now that we've stopped, she admits how much pain she's in. Lori makes Chera pull off her boot, and then Lori grabs hold of Chera's ankle and tells Chera to tell her when it hurts.

"It hurts now," Chera says immediately.

"No, wait until I wiggle it and then tell me," Lori says. So Lori waggles and pulls and pushes the ankle around in small circles.

"Right there! Right there!" Chera grunts.

Lori tries to pinpoint the pain. "Here?" Position one.

"Yes."

"Here?" Position two.

"Yes."

"Here?" Position three.

"Oh, yes."

Lori shakes her head. "I don't think it's anything serious."

"But it hurts all over," I say.

"Let's wrap it up tight and try that," Lori says. "Get some pressure on it."

While Lori loops the Ace bandage around Chera's bare ankle, I maneuver around to get a photo that will capture her hurt ankle, her pained expression, Lori wrapping the bandage, and maybe a bit of Crater Lake as a backdrop. Chera says, as a reminder of our purpose here, "I'm making it to the top." She sees me aim the camera and tries to smile. *Click.*

"There's no way I'm *not* making it to the top."

"If you're hurt," I tell her, waggling the camera, "you don't have to smile."

"Sorry."

"A couple more for Mom," I say. *Click, click.* Chera twists her face into an image of pain. "Good. Real good," I say. "So realistic."

The wrapping seems to help. At least she walks without limping.

"Now the climb gets tough," Larry tells us. Pointing to a peak, he says, "That's it. That's where we're going." Larry is like the *Reader's Digest* version of mountaineering: start in the valley, climb, climb, summit. What else is there you need to know? "First we'll go up to that saddle," he says. He swings his arm from the peak to a dip that's between the summit we're heading for and another smaller one to the left. It looks like a saddle, so I figure that one out. "Then we follow the saddle up to the summit." He swings his arm back. That distance, so easily and quickly covered by a simple wind-shield-wiper move with hand and arm, will take us about three hours. And one of the reasons it's going to take so long, Larry tells us, is because from here on up there's no trail. "It's sort of a scramble now," Larry says.

Scramble? Nothing about that word in the context of mountain climbing sounds good to me. I'm worried about Chera trying to scramble with her hurt ankle. "I'll carry your pack, Chera," I say. But Patrick is closer, and he has the pack in his hand already.

"Really, I'm okay," Chera says in protest, rising to her feet.

Patrick and I stand there, the pack between us. *Can we slice it in half?*

"You carry it up," I say, "and I'll carry it down." I've just created a compromise that I believe is very wise and Solomon-like. But even as I'm saying this bit of wisdom, I realize that Patrick has the tougher duty going up.

Instead of saying anything, I hand him the pack. I'm the adult, after all.

Handing me the carp as I stood there next to the tackle box, Dad said, "Here, this is yours." I didn't understand this plan. "First, we'll go back home and I'll fish out that bluegill from the spring," he continued, "the one I caught last week. Then we'll go to the weigh-in station and turn them both in." I didn't say anything, but the look on my face must have made him feel uncomfortable as I stood there holding that lie, feeling every twitch of the carp like a tingling electrical charge that transferred up the stringer and into my hand and arm. Dad tried to explain, "I mean, we did catch them. It's not like somebody else gave them to us." He reeled in a line, inserted a hook draped with a limp and glistening worm into one of the rod eyelets, and then turned the handle on the reel just enough to pull the slack line taut. The rod bowed slightly, and he laid it on the ground and did the same with the next one. When he was finished, he walked to the truck carrying four rod-and-reels. I followed in his steps, dangling in one hand a feisty four-pound carp and in the other a tackle box that slapped against my leg with every step. What he'd said made good sense to me.

Scramble is another word for *crawl*, I find out (quickly becoming my strongest move). And Larry is right about there not being any trail. He also advises us to spread out just in case we kick any stones loose and they tumble down, which is good advice because that happens more than once. A stone the size of a toaster oven bounces past me and ricochets at crazy angles off the other boulders. I immediately look for Chera, but she's okay. Patrick's okay too.

Most of the stones are large, as big as a washer or dryer or any other major appliance. Some stones are stacked, as if by stone masons; others are buried, and their sharp, dangerous points protrude out like medieval weapons. Others are piled in heaps, like rubble left after the collapse of a giant stone structure—a coliseum, maybe.

Find a handhold, find a foothold, find a handhold, find a foothold. "Scramble"—all the way to the saddle. Patrick and I ask Chera how she's doing so often that she starts to cut us off in midsentence with a crisp, curt, "I'm fine!"

Scramble. Scramble. Scramble.

I left my GPS at base camp, which means Chera is the only one with an altimeter in the group. Every time we stop for a gulp of water or air, or both, more than one person will ask, "So what's it on now, Chera?" She studies the watch on her wrist as we all watch her and anticipate the announcement. "Thirteen thousand eight hundred!" she says this time.

"Yay!" the chorus rises up.

"We're getting close! We're getting close!" someone calls out. "Just how close are we?" this same person asks.

Someone else does the math and announces, "Six hundred more feet."

Scramble. Scramble. Scramble.

One by one we make it to the saddle, and one after another we do the same thing: gasp. *Saddleback is a good name for this spot,* I think. *But, then again, so is Knife's Edge or Dizzy Spot, or We're All Gonna Die Ridge.* From this razor-sharp ridge you can look right down the other side of the mountain. One minute you're climbing and scrambling, and the next you're holding on for dear life. It's at this point, sitting on the sharp, bony spine of the saddle's back, that I believe it would be very easy to die up here—or down there. In the valley, I guess, is where you'd really die—after the fall. I've been to other places where you could fall, like Mammoth Cave, Niagara Falls, or the power-generating plant back home, and those places have rails, bright yellow rails, to keep you from falling, so you can lean out as far as you want to check out the view. But not here. I don't lean in any direction. I just hug the rocks. Chera's right behind me, not quite to the ridge yet, and I'm worried about her.

"Chera, are you—"

"I'm fine!" she says. She thinks I'm worried about her foot.

"Yeah?" I say. "Well, wait till you get up here. Hang on tight and keep moving." Which is impossible to do, but she knows what I mean.

The ridge is easier to follow. There's almost a trail here. From behind I hear both Chera and Patrick gasp. And sure enough, they find a way to hug rocks and keep moving. I knew they would. I wait for them to catch up and then let them pass so I can follow them to the summit, which is close, so very close.

At the top of Blanca Peak, there's no souvenir shop or hamburger stand or bathroom. As a matter of fact, there's barely enough room for all of us.

We crowd in close together and dance around and jump on the stamped-down strip of land shaped like a Y. Everyone has brought a Snickers bar, and so we eat them now and drink some of the trout water. It's windy here, and there are a few clouds in the sky, but where there are no clouds you can see forever. I spot a teenager, pivoting on one foot, turning slowly all the way around, capturing the images in his memory.

We're on the summit for only about a half hour. *All that work,* I think, all the pushing and scrambling, torture sometimes, to make it here—here to a place where our small group of people can barely move around without bumping into one another. We must have at least a dozen disposable cameras with us, so everyone is clicking, and different groups form—best friends, camp workers, troubled teens, Chera and me—and pose, and since we're so high (higher than anything around us), it's hard to get something in the background besides clouds. But that's okay, because when the pictures come back, we'll know. I ask about her ankle one more time. Then I take her pack from Patrick, because it's my turn to carry it.

But the celebration with the Snickers bars and the pictures isn't over: we also have sausage. The same sausage I had said no to at twelve thousand feet now looks and smells like filet mignon. Larry has rolls and rolls of it in his backpack, and he begins passing them out with perfect football spirals. There isn't enough for every person to have his or her own roll, so we sit close, spotted around on giant rocks, and pass the processed sausage as if it were communion. We stare at lakes below that look like puddles in a neglected sandbox, with tufts of grass pushing through the brownish gray sand.

Then, as several people in the lower country had warned us, an afternoon storm rolls in, and we scamper down quickly. We find out that scrambling backward is just as tough as going forward. Chera does much better going down. Lori, however, is battling a severe case of altitude sickness. She turns a deathly pale white, and whenever we stop to rest, she lies down, her hands cupped on her chest in a burial position. There's one big, tall boy, whom I've grown fond of, named Ben. He's slow and lanky and moves across the loose stones like a marionette, causing me to think he's going to spill forward and be gone off the other side of the mountain at any moment. For now, Ben defies all the laws of gravity, flailing and slapping across loose scree. I have to turn my head and stop watching because I'm tired of gasping so much.

No one has waited for us at Crater Lake. And a cold, blowing rain chases us all the way to Blue Lakes, where Lori quickly baptizes Patrick—a surprise to the rest of us, but something they'd been planning since the day before. Lori wades into the crystal clear water first, up to her waist, and then Patrick tiptoes in and howls some awful elk-like howl as the water moves up his body. Lori places one hand over Patrick's trembling hands, which are cupped to his chest, grabs hold of a tuft of his hair at the nape of his neck, says a quick prayer, and then dunks the boy under. He slips under quietly but then bursts up through the surface with a roar, spitting glacier water and praising the Lord. We clap thunderously and then politely turn our backs while Patrick changes his clothes.

Back at camp the people who made it to the summit share their stories with the ones who'd lain in their tents all day, napping. The nappers claim they'll never forget this day either. But when we ask them, they admit that no one there took pictures. We did.

We camp one more night at Lake Como, and this one is the worst for me yet. I'm still cold, and I can't breathe through my nose—just like the other nights, only now I'm stiff and my shins hurt. It's late, late in the night. Patrick is snoring again next to me. The tent seems to have gotten smaller. It's so small I can't stretch out like I'd like to, and my arms take turns falling asleep. Now I'm lying on my back, miserable, breathing through my mouth, when Patrick, sound asleep, rolls over and drops his hand in to mine. *Oh no.* I cough. I grunt. I pull loose and hide my hands in my sleeping bag. I roll over on to my side until my nose is pressing up against the cold canvas. Patrick, oblivious to anything of the waking life, grunts and flops over the other way. I'm just about to crawl out of the tent and go sit under a tree (I figure I can be just as miserable there) when something incredible happens. I hear this small explosion, but only *I* can hear it because it takes place inside my head. Something has broken loose. Air begins to flow. I can breathe! And, oh, I'm *so* tired. So I sleep. And not even Patrick's snoring can keep me awake.

The next morning we eat Pop-Tarts for breakfast again. I carry my strawberry-frosted tart from the shade of the pine trees to a band of warm sunshine down by the lake. I watch the trout rise and dimple shaded water the color of oil. I hear something from behind and turn to see Chera. Her ankle is all better. She doesn't limp at all. She's brought her own tart, and for a bit, we talk about Pop-Tarts, marmots (those big furry animals that live high up on mountains and pop up suddenly and unexpectedly from holes in the ground), a big pile of dung we discover there in the high grass (and wonder where it could possibly have come from), and the mountain-top, the summit. We can see it from where we stand there in the sun, by the lake, where trout rise all over. "We know what's up there now," she says, taking a small bite of her breakfast, alluding to the day before when we were wondering what it must be like up there.

"Yeah," I answer. It's only one word, but I try to use my most reflective tone. Then I use my most reflective sigh and continue, "And knowing what's up there will affect how we live down here."

She studies the summit and then looks to me and says, "Yeah, I read that quote too." Lori had given everyone a small journal, and in the front is the quote that I had just stolen.

"But I believe it," I say.

"Yeah," she agrees. "Now I understand it."

I tell her about Patrick's trying to hold my hand in the tent last night and she laughs. "Of course he doesn't know this," I say.

"I can't wait to tell him," she says and giggles.

But she does wait. We stand for a long time. The only movement we make is to eat more of our tarts. We stand there, staring at the summit of Blanca Peak, with marmots popping up all around us like those critters in that Whac-a-Mole game, trout rising behind us, mist rising behind us, sun rising behind us, people stirring in camp. We stand there as if in anticipation of that affected perception, whatever that may be.

Chera, staring at the summit, is still giggling, but I don't have to wonder why.

We drive a few hours north and spend two days in the valley before we climb our second mountain that week. It's been four days since I've bathed, and with the exception of Patrick taking a baptismal plunge at Blue Lakes, it's been eight days since anyone else has showered. But tonight we're staying in a real campground—not on a rocky trail on the side of a mountain—a campground with toilets and showers. So instead of setting up camp when we first get there, we sort of dump everything out on to the ground and then race to the hot showers and form a line, hoping the hot water holds out.

From out of nowhere a hailstorm blows across the valley and pounds our bags and tents and clothes, and there's nothing we can do about it. Then as quickly as it came, the storm's gone and is replaced by warm sunshine that dries things out in only a few moments. You'd never know there'd been a storm, except that the vans appear cleaner. Typical Colorado weather, I'm told, while waiting for a shower. "Looks like it might even rain some more," I say to a big man in a cowboy hat, just making conversation.

"You try to predict the weather around here," he drawls, "and you're either one of two things." I'm listening. "A visitor or a fool."

"I'm up from Tennessee," I answer, sounding more Southern than I normally do.

While we're in the valley, we tour Estes Park and I think about a friend of mine who was here in 1976 when the Big Thompson flood washed out the canyon and close to one hundred fifty people lost their lives. I think about this because along the roadway are small rectangular signs that direct people to climb uphill—to a higher point—if the rains ever swell the small mountain streams and flow over into the town—like they did then.

That night we set up camp in Rocky Mountain National Park. It's too dark to see the beauty. And big, cold drops of rain begin to fall from a felt-black sky. Larry moves quickly and drags a giant blue tarp from the van, and I help him tie it to some trees and stretch it over three picnic tables we've placed end to end. I see Chera scurrying from the van with a tall stack of paper bowls and a fist full of plastic spoons. Someone else fires up a stove and begins to heat a big pot of chicken noodle soup. The smell is heavenly. And that's when the sky opens up. It's too crowded under our makeshift awning, so I sprint out into the dark, into the rain, to the lighted bathrooms close by. Here it's dry—smelly, but at least dry. *But I can't stay in here all night,* I think. Plus, other campers are coming and going, and I'm starting to feel self-conscious standing here in the men's room in my raincoat, so I step out and from beneath the bathroom eaves and watch the rain. It's late and I'm hungry and my tent is floating somewhere under the pine trees. I'm so miserable here in the low country. The humidity chills my neck. The smell of wet pine needles fills my nose. I remember those rectangular signs on the side of the road back at Estes Park, and I wonder if people are moving to higher ground yet. I'm also wondering if maybe *we* should forget the blue tarp and start moving to higher ground—get out of this valley—when I hear the singing.

"I could sing of your love forever…"

I follow the voices, like a mouse to the piper, although I already know where the singing's coming from. I can't pick out Chera's voice, but I know hers has to be mixed in there. She probably even started it. I push in under the big blue tarp just enough to keep my head dry. I feel my boots filling with rain. Rain pounds the tarp so hard at times that we have to shout our praises in order for God, or one another, to hear. Finally, as the soup comes to a boil, the rain slows to a steady tapping over our heads. The soup is ready. Like an assembly line, we pass full bowls of hot liquid around the table until everyone has some. We pray. We empty them. Then we fill them and pass them again, trying to keep up with the same bowl we had before, but it really doesn't matter. That night the chicken soup becomes legend.

That night, in the valley, the rain stops and the whole camp, even Patrick and me, sleep like babies.

We're up before the sun, but it's still light enough that we can see how to pack our tents and open our Pop-Tarts. Chera has the job this morning of stacking the thin foam mats we sleep on. She stands in the back of the trailer and takes one mat, about two feet by four feet and an inch thick, and places it on a shelf about waist high. Then she begins to stack them one on top of another. Soon the pile is so high (and some of the mats are twisted and warped so they won't lie flat) that it starts to tilt over. She braces it all with a forearm, pushes back, and slings up yet another one. But the column of blue foam grows with her every effort until the stack sways and looks as if it will break at the top, like a wave or surf, and pound her from above. Before I can move to help her, Chera turns her back to the foam and, with sneakers finding purchase on the metal floor, drives backward against the stack until it strikes the wall with a leveling force. She steps away slowly to survey her work. Then she slings another mat on top and seems to almost dare it to cause trouble. She'll not coddle the sleeping mats.

We're going to climb Mount Audubon today—about thirty miles from Estes Park. This mountain is located in the Arapahoe National Forest, in the northern part of Colorado, not far from Boulder. Mount Audubon is a stumpy, bald mountain about thirteen thousand five hundred feet tall and quite blunt compared to Blanca Peak. We stand in the parking lot at the trailhead as fingers of gold sunlight break through trees to stripe the pavement. *Everyone* climbs today. No one stays in a tent and sleeps. We line up in the fingers of light like a high-school marching band on the hash marks of a football field. The Pop-Tarts are so good.

The trailhead, at eight thousand feet, is at one of the highest altitudes of any other Colorado mountain trailhead. When the sun finally rises enough to brighten Mount Audubon, couched there between two higher, more pronounced peaks, it shines like an egg yolk. And once again Larry tells us the plan. "That's the one we're going up," he says, pointing to the yellow dome. "Let's go." And Larry is off.

The trail up Mount Audubon is smooth and easy compared to what we've been through. We go the first mile, and it seems as if we're racing up. Chera's ankle is as good as new, and so she carries her own pack and pushes us all on—even me.

We rise above the tree line quickly, and I like hiking in the golden baldness because it's so warm. Only it's not so bald as it first appears. There are very few trees, but there's more grass than anywhere else we've seen, which marmots love. The big open expanse of grass reminds me of a movie. I try

to sing, *"The hills are alive..."* I don't finish because I'm waiting for someone with a better voice to finish for me. But these are teenagers, and I don't
think any of them have ever seen *The Sound of Music.*

As we move closer to the summit, we see that the peak is more like a
separate knob that rests on the bald spot. The peak reminds me of the knot
that wells up on the head of a cartoon character who gets whacked with a
baseball bat. "That's where we're going," Larry says and points again. We
stop at the base of this knob, and again Larry informs us that this is where
the trail ends—so it's time to scramble this egg yolk. And like seasoned
climbers, we spread out and crawl our way to the top.

From time to time we stop and gaze out over valley and peaks—me,
Chera, and Patrick.

"Come on, Ben," Chera calls. "Don't give up!" And the tall, gangly
teenager straightens up to answer and wobbles like he might tip over
backward.

I try singing (sort of) again, *"The hills are alive..."*

"Dad, why do you keep doing that?"

"Keep climbing," I answer.

"Want me to carry your pack, Chera?" Patrick asks.

"I'm *fine!*" Chera says.

After about five hours of climbing, we make it to the summit, where
the wind is so strong we can barely stand. But at least we all fit. This summit is flat and spread out, and if it weren't so windy, we could have a picnic up here. We huddle behind makeshift wind shelters made from
rocks—and are there ever plenty of those. Mount Audubon is a giant rock
pile. And because we need more room for all of us to sit, we form a line
and pass rocks as if they're bowls of chicken noodle soup and pile them in
a large C shape that will hide us from the wind.

We stay here on this mountaintop for over an hour—singing songs, reading scriptures, and reciting in unison the third chapter of Ecclesiastes ("There is a time for everything, and a season for every activity under heaven: a time to be born...").

We dance around, because we're happy and because we're cold. Someone snaps a picture of Chera and me, and I realize that we're both wearing the same shirts we'd worn on Blanca Peak three days before and that we're posing the same way.

"We've got to start wearing tags or signs," Chera suggests.

"All these mountaintops start looking alike after a while, don't they?" I say.

"All the campsites are sure different, though."

And I think about that. The mountaintops we call *great*. They're high. And we can see forever—but it's always tiny stuff, far away. Our hearts pound and we feel happy. With the exception of the Snickers bars and the sausages, there's not a lot of detail on the mountaintop. But in the valleys, we remember details: the flood-warning signs, rain, mud, cold, clogged sinuses, lumpy bedding, cold noodles, twisted ankles, switchbacks that don't seem to end, slimy stuff sneezed into the palm of your hand. But up here—it's truly "great" and the details from below are suddenly tiny, small, and even insignificant. We enjoy it while we can.

On the way down Chera walks ahead a little, but with Patrick. That's okay. I'll pass them by on some of the switchbacks later and I'll ask if she's doing okay, and she'll ask if I'm doing okay, and I'll give her a thumbs-up.

Just before we leave the grassy hills and drop below the tree line, I try one more time: *"The hills are alive..."*

"...with the sound of music. Aaaaah-haaaaa-ha!" From way behind me, pulling up the rear and singing a lovely soprano, it's Larry.

Since that's all the words either of us knows, that's all we sing. But it's enough for now. (And it does a good job of freaking out the teenagers.)

Sometimes, when you're headed down, back below the tree line, back into the valley where the details grow clear, it's good to sing in a falsetto voice and pretend that you're a part of a family like the von Trapps.

Especially when you're taking on Mount Rainier in a couple of weeks.

I say good-bye to Chera as she kneels by a stained lake to wash out a break-fast dish. Rose is standing next to her and comes over and gives me a big hug. I'm catching a plane back to Tennessee, but Chera is riding in the van because she's a junior counselor. She probably won't be home for a couple of days. Chera thanks me for coming out and gives me a hug with one arm about my waist, while she holds a metal plate dripping with eggs and dirt in the other. (We use dirt to clean the dishes before we rinse.) I feel so awkward saying good-bye to her. Back up at the camp, I told Ben good-bye, shook his hand. I told Alvin good-bye, slapped him on the back (careful *not* to shake his hand). I told Patrick good-bye. I even told Cindy and Heather good-bye, who were getting closer every minute to a fistfight over tent fold-up duties.

I used to give Chera rides around the room on my shoulders. Used to hold her on my hip and before a mirror where we'd play *The Pierce Family Show.* Why is it so awkward now to give her a hug and to tell her to take care and to call home and to eat well and don't talk to strangers (and good luck with Rose)? How come? Why is it such a challenge to be honest with her?

My dad netted the giant bluegill from the icy cold spring it'd been living in for the last week. The fish was hale and hearty and beat the ground with his tail to show us. Even the hook mark on his lip had already healed. We put him in a bucket with the carp and carried them to the final weigh-in at the fishing rodeo.

There were a lot of entries, but no one in the under-fourteen division had caught a fish as big as my carp. And neither had anyone caught a bluegill as big as the one Dad lifted by the lip from the cold, cold water of the bucket. We won some good prizes for our catches, and neither of us said a word to anyone about what really happened, not until I wrote it all down one day in a book I was writing about my daughter and me.

It strikes me now that I've always had a difficult time talking about what weighs down my heart. I want to be honest. But keeping quiet is easier. And something from long ago tells me that keeping quiet is better.

I don't want to do that anymore.

I climb in my rental car and drive away. I see her for a long time because she's there in the bottom of a what used to be a big lake, but the water level is so low now it's more like a giant, muddy bowl, with just a little water in the bottom. No trees or bushes around to cover her. And that haircut makes her look so grown up. She's not a little girl anymore. She's kneeling there by the water, scrubbing dishes. But before I'm gone she raises a plate and waves at me. I wave back. And I leave her there in the muddy basin, a place that reminds me of Big Bluff Creek from my childhood. I don't want to do this, but I have a plane to catch.

And I curse my lazy vocal cords.

5

The Bright Valley

Chera overlooks some serious
switchbacks on Pikes Peak.

I 'm bushed. As I sit on the plane from Colorado, everything seems to set up—joints, muscles, even cartilage. Nothing wants to work anymore. With a great expenditure of energy I pick up my Jeep from the parking lot and drive home, choosing the highway instead of the interstate. It's after ten but still warm, so different here at seven hundred feet in the South than it is at twelve thousand feet in the mountains. I'm steering with my right hand and making wavy motions with my left in the onrushing wind when I notice blue lights ahead in the little town of Smyrna that I have to pass through to get home. Three, four, maybe five police cars are in the median of the four-lane highway. Officers are out of their cars, stopping traffic and checking licenses. I fish out my wallet (*Oh, my lower back!*) and find it. I hand it to the officer.

"Everything okay?" I ask.

The young officer quickly examines my license beneath a flashlight, then hands it back. "Did you happen to come through here at this time last night?" he asks.

I shake my head. "No sir." I don't tell him I was on a mountain this time last night.

"Someone held up the Captain D's last night," he says, tipping his head in the direction of the fast-food fish restaurant right behind him. The lighted signs are bright.

"Anyone hurt?"

"Three people were killed. Shot. Just trying to find someone who may have seen anything—anything at all." He searches my face, hoping for something.

I shake my head. "Sorry."

He waves me on through. "Have a good night."

I drive on. Not making wavy motions with my hand any longer. In the rearview mirror I see the blue lights whirling. I see yellow headlights and ruby brake lights. I see the Captain D's sign on top of the building where three people died just last night.

I am back in the valley, where bright, colorful lights don't necessarily mean things aren't terribly sad. And I'm aware that tragedy can strike any-where, even up on a heavenly mountain, and I'm all the more disappointed in myself for leaving Chera without more than half a hug.

6

The Frozen Octopus

Chera can't hide the sadness she feels
after we fail evaluation at Mount Rainier.

I 'm packing the night before we fly from Nashville to Seattle, packing some of our normal mountain climbing stuff, stuff we'd used only two weeks before in Colorado, like a pocketknife (a small one this time), some string (you can do all sorts of stuff with string), and some gorp—good ol' raisins and peanuts. And then I pack some new things, things I hadn't thought about taking on any other hike, only now we were going up a glacier—must be cold. So I pack some gloves made of seal skin (not really, but the packaging compares them to seal skin because they shed water so well); an emergency blanket, which is some folded foil, sort of like the little squares I'd bring home from school after unwrapping my bologna sandwiches; and some blue underwear (long sleeved and long legged). As blue as a swimming pool—no, bluer. As blue as billiard chalk—no, bluer. I can't think of anything blue enough right now.

"Since we're going to be hiking on ice," I tell Chera, handing her a blue square neatly wrapped in plastic, "I figured you'll need a pair too." She likes the shirt. She likes the color. As blue as…

We check and double-check our backpacks before tying them up tight.

"Gloves?"

"Got 'em."

"Thermal socks?"

"Got 'em."

"Sock hat?"

"Yep."

"Crampons?" (Shoe-shaped frames with long spikes you strap to the bottoms of your boots, and although I've never used them, they tell me it's the only way you can climb a glaciated mountain.) At the mention of crampons, her hand goes to a blue pouch about the size of a shaving kit that she has cinched down to the outside of her pack. When she presses down against the canvas, I can see the impression of half a dozen steely spikes. At the proper moment, she'll withdraw these from the pouch and attach them as necessary prostheses, and they'll help convey her through the snow, over the ice, to the summit.

I didn't hear *check* this time, although it was obvious the crampons were there. (She'd tried them on in the living room the Christmas before. "Watch my carpet!" her mom had said. "Walk lightly, Chera," I'd added, knowing that probably wouldn't make much difference, but it made her mom feel better. And in the three steps she took, we both could tell they were going to work just fine.)

Chera looks up at me from her pack, her hand still resting on the spikes, muted by the canvas, and says, "Dad, this is a serious hike."

All I can do is grin, not because anything's funny or cute, but because I've felt this way for a while now. I remember when that overwhelming sense of adventure—grown-up adventure—risk, and even danger first hit me: while I was purchasing our blue, blue underwear.

We check our bags and packs at the airport, and I give Chera her boarding pass when she suddenly freezes. Then slowly, as if pointing to a bird we've been watching and she's afraid it might fly away, she points to the ceiling— no, just the air, the music in the air, actually.

"It's *Delirious!*" she says. I know this is a music group she listens to. And the music isn't coming through any speakers. Right now it's thin and far away, and Chera cants her head a bit, her pointing finger still aimed upward, using it to home in on the source. She takes a step.

I tuck my boarding pass in my pocket and follow her. Across the concourse we see a group of people, some sitting on the floor, some in airport seats that are bolted to the floor, some sitting confidently on the backs of the airport seats (confident because the seats are bolted to the floor).

They're teenagers. One young man strums a guitar while the others sing and clap. Most people walk on by—got planes to catch; some have stopped to listen. We stop too. Chera pushes up closer to the edge and begins to clap. I hang a couple of steps back and assume a more parental position, wrist in hand behind my back, at ease.

The young man playing the guitar sees Chera and asks, "You know Delirious?" Chera nods in time with the guitar music. He begins to sing again. For the next song the young man passes the guitar off to a different person. More people stop to listen. We're in Nashville, so some think that perhaps a big star has decided to put on a free concert—you know, like the Beatles that day on the rooftop. They stop long enough to see it's only a bunch of teenagers playing Christian music and then move on, to catch planes, to take care of business.

Two pilots in uniform stop next to us—in the adult section—to listen. They both nod their heads. And at the end of one song, the one closest to me shouts, "Praise God!" and applauds. *In case of rapture,* I think, *there's at least one plane going down.*

Now someone's passing the guitar to Chera. She accepts it with a smile and slips the strap over her head and borrows a pick from someone else. She makes a C chord then an A chord, smiles, and says to the group, "Know this one?" and she plays a Caedmon's Call song. I've heard her play it dozens of times at home. But now she has a chorus of twelve, and at least two airline pilots, clapping time. The teens sing louder now—however, people still pass on by, too busy. Not interested. No can do.

Chera passes the guitar off to the next person. It's almost time for us to board, but we stay for one more song, one by Michael W. Smith. I clap and mouth the words I know. At my church we project the words on the wall, and I miss that here in the airport. We belt out the chorus: *"To see you high and lifted up..."* And then we naturally (without a director) soften our voices, prayerlike, and sing, *"Holy, holy, holy."*

The player strums the final chord, and we say good-bye. We learn this group's from Kentucky and that they're going to Belize to help construct buildings. We tell them we're going to climb a mountain. The young man who owns the guitar promises to pray for us, and we tell him we'll pray for their work too.

Even though it's a five-hour flight to Seattle, there are no movies. So I read, talk some with strangers, talk with Chera, and play that last song over and over in my head—especially the last part about seeing God—on the plane and on the shuttle, as we head to the base of Mount Rainier.

We first catch a glimpse of the mountain on the plane, and even though it's impressive—huge and white and cold looking—it's too distorted, too irregular, too spread out, the "frozen octopus" I read about in that poem.

From where we are, we can't pinpoint the summit. We watch it pass beneath us for as long as we can. We try to scoop it all together, try to sweep it into a pile with our minds so we can finger the summit, so we can trace on the Plexiglass windows of the plane some sort of a route that will take us from the base to the top. But there isn't enough time. We pass over, and soon everything is green once again. Summertime.

On the shuttle, still an hour from camp, our driver, a tall, wiry young man, navigates us and others out of the Sea-Tac Airport, through a bubble of haze that has enveloped the city, until we first catch a glimpse of that frozen monster from highway level. We say the obvious:

"There's the summit."

"You think?"

"Big, huh?"

"Lots of snow."

"Can you believe it's August?"

"Glad we brought some long underwear."

But the small talk doesn't quite help calm our nerves in the imposing shadow of Mount Rainier.

Because our driver takes us along the twisty, hilly route to camp, the mountain passes around us in a circle, like Pikes Peak had around our cab; first it looms on the right side of the shuttle, then the left—more impressive than a David Copperfield trick.

The shuttle drops us off at Whittaker's Bunkhouse where, two months ago, I'd made reservations. Compared to a tent on a slope and a tree for a toilet, this is nice. We've got two beds, a bathroom, and an air conditioner.

Next door is a gift shop. We check it out and find all sorts of souvenirs—

videos, hats, T-shirts, books, lots of books about people getting stuck on mountains and barely making it out alive, sans fingers and toes and maybe a nose or ear.

This "living dangerous" mentality is hard for me to understand. At Disney World you can buy stuffed Mickeys and Donalds and so on, but they don't sell books about all the people, if any, who have died at Disney or maybe got stuck on the "It's a Small World" ride and made it out only after having a finger lopped off by one of those mechanical stunted singers. That sort of threat against safety, threat against life, doesn't bring people back to the park. But that works for Mount Rainier. Go figure.

Chera and I settle in our room, which means we prop our backpacks against the wall, and then we hike down the highway to a restaurant someone in the gift shop told us about. We're in the Pacific Northwest, and the weather is beautiful—and everyone is quick to point this out to us and to use the beauty of this day as a foil to all the miserable days that have come before it.

"Wow, is it ever a gorgeous day—not like last week when it rained every day."

"Oh, we count ourselves lucky when it's bright and sunny like this and not so gray and dreary like it usually is."

We appreciate the sunny sky, and part of me hopes it isn't going to melt the mountain away before we get there. We can't see it any longer from where we're staying. "Must not be that big," I say to Chera and laugh, knowing I'm wrong. But the day after tomorrow we'll confront the mountain, so from a safe distance, out of view and hiking down a busy highway toward a greasy restaurant, you could say I launch the first salvo.

We sleep that first night without any air conditioning, just the fan on low for the soft, constant hum. We wake up a bit excited, a bit nervous. Today we go to the mandatory climbing school. This is where we learn about using an ice ax and crampons and how to wear the three different pairs of mittens they gave to me when I picked up all the other rental gear.

"You think it's in case one pair gets dirty?" I ask Chera, stuffing the mittens into my pack. I'm only sort of kidding.

"I think it's going to be cold," she answers. *But it's been sunny the last two days,* I think. *Hot.*

We fill our packs—way too heavy—and jump on the same shuttle bus that had brought us from the airport for another thirty-mile ride, this time up to Paradise—the town, that is—tucked into the forest, in the side of a hill, at the base of The Mountain. It's a nice, quaint mountain lodge with lots of dark cedar and pine beams, and Chera wonders why we didn't stay here. I shrug and say, "Never got the brochure."

Someone who works there, another tall, wiry kid, points us up a path to the equipment house, where we'll meet our guide. About sixteen of us hoist our packs up onto our backs and, like nervous turtles, hike up a paved path to a gabled building called the guide house—where most everyone walks about in big plastic boots. And if you haven't put yours on already, you feel as if you've stepped into the land of the giants. In the guide house, open and roomy with rows of benches so you can sit down and buckle your buckles, everyone is suddenly tall and wiry.

We're still too close to the mountain to see the summit, but we can see its eastern face, catcher of the morning sun, most-photographed profile. We saw this image in the airport on the front of a vending machine that sells water. We saw it on a calendar in the restaurant we ate at just last night. We saw it on the fronts of T-shirts and disaster books in the gift shop. It's also on every license plate of all the local cars.

Massive. Overwhelming. Not real. Too real. Those are words I think of. *We're looking at it through a magnifying lens,* I think. It's bigger than big.

Bigger than you can imagine or I can describe. All the tall, wiry people look short!

We first meet our guide after we pull our boots on, just outside of the guide house. He tells us his name is Huey, a good name to have when lots of people call your name out all day long: *Huey, where are we going? Huey, is this how you wrap an ice ax wound? Huey, aren't we there yet?* He's a bit older than I am, midforties probably, and of course, he's tall and wiry. He tells us to circle around, to listen up, and so we all kick and scoot our packs closer and surround him.

"Is everyone here for the climbing school and evaluation?" he asks. He has a high-pitched voice, made higher because he's trying to project out to our circled group. Chera looks at me when she hears the word "evaluation." She's only sixteen, still living daily in a world of pop quizzes and exams, where nearly every day she's evaluated and analyzed and categorized. It's a nervous look she gives me, uneasy. *A bit intense,* I think, *but at least not panicky.*

Huey starts to explain the day ahead of us when suddenly he stops and calls to a couple of men who have just walked out of the front door of the guide house. "Excuse me!" he calls out and adds a name, but it's not one I've ever heard before—foreign, Middle Eastern. The men stop and turn and come to Huey. The first man is older and carries a notebook under one arm. He's dark, from India or Pakistan or close by, perhaps, I think. Shorter than me but lots heavier.

"People," Huey addresses us, placing one hand upon the man's shoulder, "this is [that name I can't remember].* He is the first man to ever climb Everest *twice.*" Huey beams. He's so proud to be in this man's presence that

---

* The climber's name is Nawang Gombu; he summited in 1963 and 1965.

he begins to clap. Our circled group claps too, and although I can't see if all his toes are there, because he's wearing shoes, it's good to see that his fingers and ears and the tip of his nose are all accounted for. He is alive, he is walking, he is short and chubby. He is hope standing there before us. I clap dramatically.

Mr. (that name I couldn't pronounce probably even if I could remember it) leaves and Huey turns to address his charges. "Now our plan for today," he says, "is to strap on our packs and hike up to the snowfields, about two miles from here. That's where we'll teach you all about hiking on a glacier. Now one of the most important things you'll do out here the next few days is to put on your sunscreen. On the mountain, at this altitude [about six thousand feet now], on the snow, you'll turn into a lobster in a few minutes." Then he tells us a story about how he had turned into a lobster—on a day much less sunny than today. "*And* wear your sunglasses, glacier glasses preferably." He holds his up to demonstrate. "The kind with the little flaps on the side because even if there is just a pinhole, light can shoot in there like a *laser.*" He emphasizes "laser." He shakes his head, as if sadly remembering. Then he tells us a long story about the time he went snow blind. I wonder if it was that same day he'd turned into a lobster. He just wasn't thinking that day.

Huey introduces a couple of helpers to us: Adam and Caroline. They're two good-looking college kids, the kind who probably live on the mountain all summer and just zip to the summit every now and then to break up the day. I ask Caroline how many times she's been to the summit. "Seventeen," she says. "I've tried a lot more than that, but the weather turned us back a few times."

"So the weather can change that quick? I mean, if you watch the Weather Channel and all…"

"The mountain sort of creates its own weather," she explains as we apply sunscreen.

"Oh yeah?"

"A snowstorm can pop up just like that." She snaps her fingers, and I think that's pretty quick.

We're still outside the guide house and haven't left for the snowfields when Huey explains to all of us the proper way to grip an ice ax. First of all, let me explain a bit about the ax. It looks like a garden pick, shorter than a walking cane, shaped like a T with one side pointed like a pick and designed for stabbing the ice. The other side is flat like an ax for chopping the ice. The base also has a point on it, also designed to stab the ice. Now, if you grip tightly to the crosspiece that forms the T, you can supposedly stab the ice with the small point, and this will help you maintain your balance. I say *supposedly* because I've never held an ice ax before. And today is the first time I've seen one up close. Huey tells us a long story about all the ways the ice ax has saved his life. And, as an aside, he says all those movies where someone flies through the air and slams an ice ax into the side of a mountain, where he then proceeds to pull himself up hand over fist, is all baloney.

"An ice ax is a very dangerous tool," Huey tells us. "There's a proper grip that you'll all learn and obey. First, put the ax by your side with the point—the business end—facing behind you, thumb underneath the flat part, and grip the head of the ax right where the shaft connects with the head." He demonstrates the perfect grip, and we all follow suit. Easy. So easy. "Now if you need to switch hands, and you will, do it like this." And he passes the ax in front of him, point always behind. I do the same a couple of times and then make a few more really quick, really fast passes, sort of "toss" it from right hand to left, left to right, and the heavy metal slaps against the palm of my hand. Pass. *Slap.* Pass. *Slap.* Pass. *Slap.* Easy. Chera grins at me, but I can tell the skill level of what I've accomplished isn't high enough to impress her.

"Now there's going to come a time," explains Huey above the general clinking and slapping sounds of everyone mastering the perfect grip of an ice ax, "that you're going to get tired, your mind will wander, and you're going to get lazy. When that happens"—he lifts his ax, still in perfect grip, and, with his other hand, grasps it at its farthest-most pointed tip and releases the grip he has on the ax head. He holds it as if it's a campfire hatchet and he's about to split of piece of kindling—"you'll wind up with what we call here on The Mountain a 'tourist grip.'" He holds the ax up high now by the end of its handle and waggles it maniacally. "Don't do this!" he says, shaking the ax, his eyes like lasers and burning into each and every pair of glacier glasses. "Do this and someone could get hurt!"

Then stop doing that! I want to scream, but don't, and only squeeze my perfect grip even tighter.

He lowers the ice ax, resumes the perfect grip, and says, "Now let's get your packs on, and follow me to the snowfields."

Through neat patches of wildflowers that were surely put there by a florist only moments before we arrived, we begin to trek upward along a nice, smooth, well-maintained trail that families with children saunter along (sometimes saunter right alongside us, causing the whole "team" to scoot to one edge of the trail). The trail, always going up, runs sometimes parallel to, sometimes perpendicular to, small trickling streams—snowmelt streams, we learn. Always going up. It's two miles to the edge of the snowfield. We can only imagine...Christmastime in August?

We haven't gone very far when one of the hikers, the only other woman hiker, named Angel, drops out. She just stops walking and we leave her. "She can find her way back," Caroline says. This doesn't seem so kind.

After the first mile, we're in the middle of a series of serious switchbacks, where some of our team, from the viewpoint we have from below, appear to be walking along the tops of others' heads. Chera and I are nearly at the end of the line. Only a few people are behind us, one being sweet Caroline. But a gap of considerable distance is opening between Chera and the next person in line. By now Caroline knows all our names ("Good-bye, Angel!") and calls out from the rear, "Hey, guys, let's close up that gap! Chera, step to the side and let them around you." She does, but I think the others have been enjoying the pace Chera, and not Huey, has set. But they go around as instructed. I stick with Chera and Caroline sticks right behind me. "We have to pick up the pace, guys!" she calls. She says *guys,* but she really means *Chera.*

Chera trudges on. She looks pale, yet I ask anyway, "Are you okay?"

She breathes too hard, pants too much; her lips are dry. "I'm tired," she says, but trudges on.

I hope Caroline hasn't heard that. *We must hide her tiredness,* I think. We'll just let them know that we have to set our own pace. We're seasoned hikers now, seasoned mountain climbers. We've climbed three mountains already—two of them only three weeks before. We know what we're doing.

"Chera, we need to catch up!" Caroline calls.

I exaggerate my steps, hoping it looks as if we're going faster. But the gap between Chera and the next hiker in the team gets wider and wider. We see them above us, walking on our heads, making the switchbacks we know we have to negotiate—soon.

Caroline catches up to me and asks, in a lower voice so Chera can't hear, "How old is Chera?"

"Sixteen."

She nods. "Sixteen is still pretty young, and there's still a lot of developing of the lungs to go."

I'm defensive. "Hey, we've climbed other mountains before—*fourteeners.* And we ran a marathon back in the spring—twenty-six miles. She can do this."

Caroline doesn't even pause to consider what I'm saying. Instead she starts in with a well-practiced, chamber-of-commerce speech, one designed for third-graders. "There are lots of other trails and day hikes around here that I bet you guys will love. We'll make it to the snowfield. Don't worry, I'll get her there. And you guys will have fun at the school. And when we get back, I'll get some information about all the fun stuff there is to do around here—if you like hiking."

Chera pauses to catch her breath. I'm grateful for the stop. "Chera, can't stop!" Caroline honks. "You need to breathe harder. Pretend you're blowing out birthday candles. *Wooooosh!* Like that. Pressure breathe!"

"*Whosh.*"

"No. *Whoooooosh!*"

"*Whoosh.*"

"*WHOOOOOOOOOOOSH!*"

"So that's it?" I ask her. "We don't get to climb?"

"If you can't keep up with Huey, then he's not going to let you go."

Disappointment, dense as ice, sits in the pit of my stomach.

"And if *you* stay back," she tells me, "you'll probably fail too."

I don't know what to do. I'm disappointed, but I'm also angry. All the planning, the time, the money just to get here to hear we can't even try. But I guess this is part of the trying. I pass by Chera and on the way by attach an invisible rope to her waist. From in front I pull her along. I keep asking if she's all right, and she keeps saying yes, or nodding, expending energy to answer my dumb questions. I go to the end of a switchback and wait. I can see Huey. We're not that far behind! I tug on my invisible rope. "Let's keep moving!" peals up from below me. "Blow out those candles, Chera! Come on! Pretend you're eighty years old today and you got a big old cake full of candles! *Whooooosh, whoooooosh!*"

I'm at another turn, hiding from Caroline, still tugging on my invisible rope, when Chera stops and takes one deep breath after another. Caroline stops too. She doesn't say anything this time, doesn't push, doesn't seem to care. I know it's over, but Chera doesn't—not yet. She sees me. I'm only a few feet away. She's sweating heavily, panting, *whoosh*ing. Her hair is tied up in one of those handkerchiefs that has some sort of repeating pattern on it, the kind you wear in the great outdoors. I feel I need to tell her the trip is over.

Then, slowly, her dry lips part and she grins, painfully. It's a beautiful grin, and the ice in my stomach melts. "Well," she pants, using up more energy, "I guess I'm ready for a jog." I'm ashamed at having been angry. Respectfully, Caroline keeps her mouth shut and lets us catch our breath. No more *whoosh*ing.

Five minutes. That's how long Huey and the "team" have been there when we arrive at the snowfield. But that's too long. The rest of the group has already formed a semicircle around Huey, sitting on their packs in order to stay off the snow. We're obviously late, kick-stepping into the snow, spraying little fans before us and onto the fringes of the group while Huey gives another speech—or short talk—about how we should respect The Mountain, or maybe it's how to survive an avalanche, I'm not sure, because I'm not paying attention. I just know he's talking, and he's not so tired he can't do that. We plop our backpacks onto the snow and take a seat. The back of Chera's shirt is plastered to her skin, soaked with perspiration. I can feel a chill on my back as well. We both drink, and you can almost see it leaking out—back, armpits, temples.

Huey gives us a few minutes to hydrate, and I lean over and tell Chera, "I don't think they're going to let us climb."

She fingers her water bottle, exaggerates a frown, and shakes her head; defeated, denial, disappointment—the same shake will work for any of them. The summit is to our backs. A few moments ago, at one of the switchbacks where she had paused, we could see it plainly. "I could hardly look at it," she tells me now. "Because I knew they weren't going to let us climb, and I could see the summit and I just knew I was going to cry."

I figure it must have been the time she'd smiled and made the joke. "It's no big deal," I say. That would be easier to believe than the idea that I really do have an invisible rope.

She shakes her head again, letting me know that she doesn't believe me. "I asked God to please let me climb this mountain," she says. "But if I can't climb this time, then at least let me learn *something*." She looks into the distance, into the valley, while she takes another drink. She says what she feels, and I'm sure she hasn't leaned that from me. But I silently pray she never stops.

Huey walks back to his makeshift pulpit, swinging his ice ax in his perfect grip. Break is over.

"So why don't we play in the snow and just have some fun," I say.

"I've never played in the snow in August before," she answers.

"I've never played with an ice ax before."

We're stamping around on snow that probably fell from the sky last winter and just won't melt. Only a snowball's throw away is the Nisqually Glacier, nestled in the valley like ice will build in a gutter. In some places the ice is five hundred feet thick. This big slow beast moves only about six inches per year.

It's a sunny day and warm, so we're wearing our waterproof pants and T-shirts. Huey wants to show us how to use the ice ax, now that we're on real ice. Under his direction we pick, we chop, we flail our axes into the ice to climb, to turn, and to stop ourselves from sliding off the mountain. One at a time we sit on our rear ends and raise our boots to slide down the mountain, our slick pants *whoosh*ing over the ice, until Huey calls out "Stop!" At that point we roll over on our stomachs, stabbing the pointy side of the ax down into the snow. With big kicks we dig in with toes and crampons, knees off the ground, mashing the ax deeper into the ice, lifting on its handle for leverage. If our form is right, we finish with our rear ends high in the air, faces turned out, throats only two inches or less from the flat blade of the ax.

"Good, good," says Huey. "Kick harder, Chera," he says. "You'll have to give that handle a big pull!" Huey adds. "Come on, Chera! Be aggressive!"

Next Caroline teaches us how to walk downhill on the glacier. "You need to squat, like this," she says, and shows us the proper way to squat. She looks too funny. Once we're in a squatting position (and we all look funny), we follow Caroline by taking slow, waddling steps, digging in ferociously with each heel, leaning down the hill so that it looks as if we're about to tumble headlong into the snow. Plunge stepping, she calls it.

"Good, good," says Huey as we take turns coming down a short slope. "Dig in, Chera! Be more aggressive!" He turns to those who have already made it down and explains, "That's the problem with some of the women climbers: they aren't aggressive enough." Behind him Chera kicks hard down into the ice, and I think the glacier moves. I think.

After practicing our steps, we tie ropes about our waists and practice making switchbacks up the slope and across the glacier. "Good, good," says Huey. "Don't forget to switch hands with that rope, Chera," he adds.

Playing on the snow—with, or without, ice axes—would have been lots more fun without Huey.

We're standing around in another semicircle—the sun has drained us, the snow has whipped our legs into spaghetti—when I hear Huey call, "Pierce!"

Oh no. Now what's he going to fuss about? I'm going to have to say something now. For crying out loud! We're not even going to get to climb tomorrow and he keeps riding Chera and there's no need—

"Pierce, what are you doing?"

Is he talking to me? I look around and there's no one behind me. I guess he's talking to me. *Are you talking to me?* my body language asks. *What did I do?*

"Everyone, take a good look at Pierce…"

Guess he's about to tell me what's wrong. Everyone on the mountain looks at me.

"…and tell me what sort of grip he has on his ice ax."

Uh-oh! The head of the ax slaps against my leg. I'm hanging on to the handle. The three pointy ends are pointing in three wrong directions. The group takes a minute to size me up, while I slowly rework my grip. I'm still making that final adjustment when I hear them say, in unison, "Tourist grip!"

"That's right," says Huey, in a congratulatory tone, "a *tourist* grip." He ignores the fact that I've repaired that and am now gripping it like a seasoned mountain climber. I look at Chera and she just shrugs (a "welcome to my world" shrug), then waggles her ice ax for me so I can see what a *proper* grip looks like.

Things couldn't get any worse. That is, until I nearly kill my whole platoon. We're doing the walking-up-the-snowy-slope thing again, ropes around waists, making switchbacks, dropping to the snow and digging in whenever Huey makes even the slightest grunting noise, when I accidentally step on a rope with my crampons.

"Pierce, don't step on the rope!" he calls out, too loud for such a small group, which makes me think he's trying to make a point. I believe he's been waiting for someone to step on a rope all day.

"Folks, here's what happens when you step on a rope," Huey says, and here comes another speech. "You get a little nick on the rope. Then up on the mountain you fall down and your partners dig in to stop you. Only now your rope, the one connecting you to the rest of the group, has a little nick in it. And say the nick is up near the top, where the anchor climber is trying to dig in. It breaks and *all* of you spill into the chasm."

He looks at me, and I look at my group, my partners, my fellow climbers; and with a nod, I offer an apology for theoretically killing them all—or at least being responsible for them falling into some ice cave where they'll be forced, after the fifth day with no food, to eat the weakest person. But more than anything else, I'm sorry for the speech we have to endure, a long story about the time Huey was on some mountain and somebody stepped on the rope and nearly killed them all.

"Oops," I say, as genuinely as I can, and nudge the rope away from me, first with my crampons (before I realize that's probably not a good idea), and then with the end of my ice ax. Chera's the only one grinning.

The training is over, and Chera and I are glad to get off the snow. Glad to be going down and away from everyone. Disappointment echoes louder and longer than a Ricola commercial, where that man screams out the throat lozenge name into a valley. Only no matter what sounds go into the valley now (singing birds, kids on the lower trails with their families, people laughing and having a wonderful time enjoying God's creation), what comes back to us is "failed evaluation."

We don't say much on the way down. We don't talk about how hard it was for Chera to keep up on the trail. Or about how I almost killed everyone with my crampons and ice ax. Disappointment. Crushing disappointment.

"Well, I learned something," Chera says. She's always learning something, no matter how crushed or disappointed she is or how many people we nearly killed. There's always a lesson there.

"What's that, Chera?" I ask. I need help with this day's news.

"We can't always wing it."

I suddenly think about all the hours we *didn't* train, *didn't* prepare. Oh, we ran some and walked some. But the idea of climbing this mountain never pushed us like it should have. I had one big "tourist grip" on this whole climb. I hated the way Huey had ridden us, had shouted at us, had called us down. But even more, I hated admitting that he was right. (I still don't think I stepped on that rope, though.) And Chera knows it.

We trudge into Paradise. The irony of the lodge's name does not escape us. "Let's get some ice cream," I say to Chera after seeing someone walk by with a big cone of chocolate. Off the ice now, the heat is cooking us, and our feet, which are entombed in the big plastic boots, bake like potatoes. We sit on the pavilion of the Paradise Inn, boot buckles loose, eating our cones and waiting for the shuttle when Angel walks by. She's still wearing her glacier glasses, looking rather sporty. She brings us tidings of good news: she tells us that she hiked up to Camp Muir after she left us.

"Camp Muir?" I ask. "Isn't that base camp?"

"Oh yes," says Angel. "There were lots of people up there. Most of them going up to the summit later."

"And you just walked up there all by yourself? No guide? No fees? No special equipment?"

She nods and looks at our boots. "I wish I'd had your boots, though. It gets a little slushy along the way."

She asks about our ice-cream cones, and I point her into the lodge. Chera looks at me, I look at Chera. The wheels are turning. "Chera..."

"Yes?"

"Are you thinking what I'm thinking?"

"I'm thinking," starts Chera, "that we hike up to Camp Muir tomorrow and beat our team there. Show Huey that we can do it."

"You mean race them up?"

"No, *beat* them up."

I'm fighting the rapid melting of my ice cream now by sucking out the melt from the bottom. "You know what that means, don't you?" I say.

"What?"

"That we'll have to ride the shuttle back here in the morning—with 'the team.' Everyone will be dressed to summit, talking about climbing and summiting. We'll have to listen to all that talk and know we're not going."

She takes a deep breath, furrows her brow, presses her lips tightly together as she evaluates the scenario, then says, "So we just do it."

"Really?"

"We ride over, hop off the shuttle with our boots already on so we get a good jump on them. Then we beat Huey to base camp. That's our goal." She states this so matter-of-factly.

I grin (chocolate probably on my lips somewhere) and say, "I like it. We wave to Huey, maybe shake his hand. Tell him it was nice beating him to base camp. That's *our* summit."

"Not very nice of us, though, is it?"

I push the rest of the cone into my mouth (really too much for one bite) and say, "We'll be kind about it, you know. It's a matter of manners."

"Huh?"

"Manners."

"Oh yeah." She touches the corner of her mouth and says, "You've got something right there."

"Oh. Thanks."

The shuttle arrives and we load up to leave Paradise—for now.

Back at the bunkhouse we meet a fellow who cheers us up, and because of that, we believe that perhaps he's another angel—a cheering-up angel. His name is Rick, but he looks like Tom Green, that crazy comedian/actor. He's tall, soft-looking, has short dark hair and a goatee—like Tom. He's so friendly that immediately Chera and I like him.

"So you guys climbed The Mountain?" he asks.

"No," I say. "We—uh—we went to the school today."

"Oh, I'm doing that tomorrow. They say it's fun."

"You'll do a lot of stuff," I tell him. "In the snow."

"So you climb tomorrow?"

Chera looks at me, and we make eye contact for a full second before I say, "We're scheduled to go up tomorrow."

"So how does that work," he wants to know. "How many in your group? Are you, like, tied to each other? Is it really cold? Really slick?"

Or maybe he's the honesty angel, I think. I have to come clean. "We're not going to summit tomorrow, Rick."

"Oh?"

I take a deep breath. "We didn't quite cut the evaluation today. But we're thinking of going back and doing some…free hiking." That sounds good.

"That sounds like fun."

I think for a minute that he's going to ask to come with us. But he doesn't. We wish him the best of luck and leave. We decide to grab a bite at a restaurant that's about a mile from the bunkhouse. And since we don't have a car, we have to hike for our dinner.

No matter where we go, we can't seem to escape The Mountain. In the restaurant the menu covers have a nice photograph of Mount Rainier. "Look," I say to Chera and place my finger at the summit. "Huey's been there." Chera rolls her eyes.

"I can't believe this," Chera says, as she looks over my shoulder.

"What?"

She points to the wall behind me, and I turn to see an old circular saw blade hanging on a nail. Someone has painted The Mountain on its face. The center hole is at the base of the mountain, about where we failed evaluation only hours before.

I turn back around. "Oh no, look at that," I say to Chera. I point to my cloth napkin on the table. It's clumped and shaped just like Mount Rainier.

Chera shakes her head. "We have to come back," she says. "We have to do this."

So the mountain's image, plastered, etched, and engraved on everything from shot glasses to jukeboxes, is no longer just a pretty picture. It's become a clear call to return, to focus for an entire year on nothing but this mountain, its summit. To run. To train (for real, this time). To renew our membership at the gym. *Urrrggh!* I reach over and flatten the napkin with my hand—and it's not a quick smack or a *whop!* either. I squash the summit with my palm slowly, bringing my hand down and crushing the napkin-mountain as if it were an aluminum can and I, a giant aluminum-can compactor. Chera doesn't grin or smile, but watches me, steely eyed, and together (before the waitress can set down the mashed potatoes that will probably somewhat resemble a mountain peak) we commit to the challenge together. We agree to come back, this same time next year. To climb. To summit.

We jump on the shuttle at 7 a.m. with our plastic boots on and ski poles in hand and carrying only some light daypacks. Some from our group the day before are there, carrying much heavier stuff. They don't know about us yet (that we didn't make the cut), so I explain that we're just going for a hike, we won't be climbing. And as much as I want to tell them all that we'll be back here same time next year, I don't. They're heading up The Mountain this morning and will summit sometime tomorrow morning. They don't care what we're doing this time next year.

When the shuttle arrives at Paradise, we literally jump off and race up the trail. It's paved for a few hundred yards, and so we don't stop to adjust, tighten, or situate until we're several hundred yards from the pack. We're both anxious and nervous. I kick around some thoughts. *What if they pass us?* That would be the ultimate embarrassment. *What if we can't make it? Do we still wave at them on our way down? Have we let pride take over way too much of this little climb? Nah.* Let's climb.

For the next hour and a half we walk through the pages of that calendar hanging on the wall in that greasy restaurant. The trail wends through lush greenery, and wildflowers spot the mountainside like the aftermath of a paintball battle. We pass only a few patches of snow here and there, nothing big. The trail is nice and comfortable, steadily up, but not bad. These are the trails built for the day hikers, the hotel guests. And we see lots of them along the way.

At one point we stop to catch our breath, but the view keeps taking it away. The sky is completely cloudless, as blue as…I'm not sure. Something. Ahead of us is Mount Rainier. All ice and rock, monopolizing the sky. Some big woolly marmots (beavers without the flat tails) chatter and wrestle just a few feet away. The air is still warm but not dry. It's thin and feels like energy flowing into my nose and into my chest. It's so warm here that we take off our sweatshirts and strip down to our blue, blue undershirts.

"This is great, Dad," Chera says. "I'm glad we failed. I'm glad we're doing this without the big group."

Me too. I want to tell her she's safe. That no matter how big this mountain is, I'll take care of her. I don't know why I want to say that. I don't know why I don't. But at that moment I want her to know how much I care for her, how much I love her and how much…how much…how much…

We're standing on the most amazing, gigantic, colossal, great big… My built-in thesaurus is failing me, as the mountain seems to take on more and more magnitude. I want to tell her that I love her and will take care of her as much as this mountain is big—but I don't. But if she falls down, I'll catch her and she'll know how much I love her.

"I wonder what God was thinking when he made this?" Chera asks, taking in the mountain.

I shake my head and wonder too. And then I remember what we had read at Barr Camp, on Pikes Peak over a year before, and paraphrase (badly) that: "He can make the biggest mountain melt like wax."

I was only trying to demonstrate God's power, his might, to compare it to something we *can* understand, like this mountain. Oh well. Chera clicks her ski poles against the rock. It's time to climb again.

Up until now we've only passed along and through patches of snow, some brown or blackened from algae or mineral deposits, some slushy because of the sun and the constant melting. We never seem to come closer to the Nisqually Glacier to our left. From this new vantage point, we see the edge, a cutaway view, blue and thick, beneath the white coating of snow, like raspberry Jell-O coated in white icing that someone has sliced with a serrated knife. Ahead of us we see snow, lots of snow, long and unbroken, dotted here and there by craggy rock outcroppings. One rock formation, higher up, looks like a castle. But there are no trees anywhere, so it's hard to draw a perspective. It seems like we could just scoot right on up, maybe even trip over Camp Muir, and we'll have to make ourselves slow down or we'll wind up at the summit. Appears that way, anyway.

We reach a stream called Pebble Creek, which is really a misnomer. It should be called Raging Cataract or Boulder Creek or Slip and Fall In and Drown Creek because it's that impressive. "This is awesome!" Chera calls out above the roar of the water. Together we plot out the best path for crossing: "Step there." "Step there." "Not there. That looks slippery." "Try to reach that one if you can." "Good luck."

The crossing is wide and dangerous, and again, like when we had reached the saddleback of Blanca Peak a few weeks earlier, we have the sense that something bad could happen here and no one would know about it for days. Chera says so, and I try to make her feel better. "Nah," I say, "you'd probably wash up somewhere at Paradise Inn. Maybe by the tennis courts."

"Makes me feel better," Chera says.

We negotiate Wash You Down to the Tennis Courts Creek and are officially on the Muir Snowfield. I'd seen it on the map earlier. "This is a famous snowfield," I tell Chera.

"Why is it famous?" Chera asks.

"Don't know, but it's on the map."

She squints upward, into the snow, wondering, like me, why it's famous. We look back, and behind us we see the peaks of three mountains, two pretty mountains and one craggy one. We wonder what they are.

"Better wear your glacier glasses," I tell Chera, as I fit mine down on my nose and press the sides in to seal out the direct light. I still remember Huey's long story about going snow blind on a fifteen-minute trip.

"I don't have my glasses," Chera says. She pats her shirt, her jacket, her pockets. Nothing. "I took them off when I took off my sweatshirt earlier. I must have left them on that rock."

That was over a mile back. There's no way they're still there. Besides, if we go back for them, we won't have time to climb to Camp Muir; we'll miss the shuttle. But if she goes without the glasses, she'll go snow blind.

"We have to go back," I say.

"I can squint," she says about heading up the glacier without her glasses.

"You heard what Huey said. Fifteen minutes and it's like red-hot pokers in your eyeballs. It's too risky."

"I'll keep my eyes closed," she says. "You can guide me. I'll follow your voice." Her mind is clicking. She's being resourceful. She's brainstorming. She loosens the bandanna from her head. "I'll wear a blindfold, like this." She cinches the cloth around her face, covering her eyes. Now she stands there, looking like a political hostage—only on a ski slope.

I consider her and her situation and her determination for a moment.

I'm the father. I'm the responsible one. I know better. We should go back. "Is any light at all coming in?" I ask.

She shakes her head—like a political hostage afraid to speak.

"Can you see anything at all?"

"I can see your shape, but I can't tell it's you," she answers.

"Chera, I don't know…snow blind, I'm telling you—"

"We *have* to make it to Camp Muir…"

Before they do, she doesn't finish, but it's understood.

I sigh, pressure breathe *(whoosh!),* and say, "Okay. Let's try a little ways. But if I think it's hurting you at all, I'm turning around." In Huey's story, he never felt a thing until twenty-four hours later, when the red-hot pokers punctured his eyeballs.

She takes a step and nearly runs into me. "Whoa, whoa," I say. "Just follow my voice and…and my…outline."

We begin up the famous Muir Snowfield, one baby step at a time, me leading the way, Chera blindfolded. The view is incredible, but I try not to say anything about it—sensitive to Chera's new disability. But I do try to talk enough so she can keep on a straight line. A few people boot ski down past us. If they see us, they don't pay much attention to my hostage. We've come maybe a half mile when I see an older man making his way down the snowfield toward us. He's maybe in his fifties, wearing a big red sweatshirt. One look at him and I can tell he's an angel. No doubt. Even before we speak.

"You guys going to Camp Muir?" he asks.

"Yeah, hopefully," I say. "How much farther?"

He turns on the slope and looks back up the way he'd just come. "That big rock there," he says, pointing to the giant, brown rock that looks like a castle, the one we had spotted earlier, "that's Gibraltar Rock. Camp Muir is at the base of it. About a mile and a half, I guess. Beautiful day for climbing," he says.

"Yeah."

"Lot better than the rain we had last week."

He looks out over the vista below us, so I ask him, "Do you know what those mountains are?"

"That's Mount Adams," he says, pointing to his far left. "The one in the middle is Mount Hood—beautiful shaped mountain. And that over there is Mount St. Helens, or what's left of her."

"Adams, Hood, St. Helens," I repeat after him and point to the peaks. I see Chera looking from beneath her blindfold, not daring to remove it totally, no doubt remembering Huey's horrific recounting of endless pain and agony. She's traveled about a half mile totally blindfolded now. The climb on the snowfield is slow and arduous, and we still have a long ways to go. *It's time to turn back,* I think—*unless, of course, this angel is willing to make a deal.* So I ask.

"Excuse me," I say, reaching for my wallet. "But would you be willing to sell me that extra pair of sunglasses you have there around your neck?" How much do you offer an angel for polarized glasses, anyway?

The angel looks to me, then to Chera (who is facing in the direction of his shape), then back to me and, realizing that we aren't the remnants of a coup-gone-bad down at Paradise Inn, says to Chera, "Oh, my dear. Please, just take these. Why…you'll go snow blind out here without glasses." And just like that he hands over the glasses and makes me put away my wallet. (I couldn't have offered him much anyway, unless he took plastic.)

Chera pulls loose the blindfold and, with a laugh, slips on the new sunglasses. "Wow!" She says about the view. "So this is what I've been missing. Let's see…" And she turns to face downhill and points to the distant peaks: "Mount Adams, Mount Hood, and Mount St. Helens," she says.

We tell our angel good-bye and continue on up to Camp Muir with renewed energy, confidence, and a sporty-looking pair of sunglasses. We laugh and talk about the encounter when suddenly Chera looks back and the angel is gone. We stop and stare at the whiteness, all smooth and empty—no one is there! This is just like all the angel stories you hear about. We hardly breathe for several long seconds—until we see the round top of a head rising in the midst of all the white. Then shoulders. Then his arms pumping up and down as he digs in with his ski poles. The big red sweat-shirt. He had only disappeared into a dip that we can't discern from where we stand.

"I still say he's an angel," Chera says. "One who likes to hike."

I trudged up through the ice and snow in a slick pair of sneakers, trying to get to the trailer Dad and I lived in at the top of a big hill that my car couldn't make in that kind of weather. We didn't usually get as much snow in Tennessee as we did my senior year in high school. I walked in to find Dad sitting in an uncomfortable kitchen chair, leaning forward with his elbows on his knees, his palms turned out to catch the red glow of the space heater in front of him. His weathered, flushed face was a close match for the glowing, radiant coils of the heater. When he was drinking like that, he could sit in front of a space heater or an open oven for hours. He was still sitting like that when I decided to go to bed. I closed the door to my room because sometimes he'd start talking and mumbling, usually about stuff that'd happened years before. If that happened, I'd never get any rest.

I fell asleep and had been asleep for quite some time when I turned at the same instant that a bright flash filled the gap at the bottom of the door. *Hmmm. Wonder what that was?* Now I was wide awake. So I threw back the covers, got out of bed, and pulled the door open. Across the room, Dad's chair was empty. Sometime in the night, as usual, he'd risen from the chair and staggered his way to bed. But I noticed there, next to the space heater, a small yellow flame licking its way up the curtains. It was no bigger than a canary and seemed harmless—playful, even. I casually walked over to the flame, bent down, and blew it out, as if it were a giant candle. The flame died instantly, leaving a red, glowing C-shape where the fire had taken a bite from the curtain. I patted the area until the red was gone and all was black and dark. Then I unplugged the space heater and went back to bed.

Later, I wondered if maybe an angel had awakened me. That would be a good sign that maybe God was starting to pay attention to me, right? Still, I couldn't be sure.

Up, up, up we trudge along the Muir Snowfield. We're taking baby steps now because it's too slippery and too steep to try to take anything bigger than that. It's so warm that we're sweating on the snowfield. The snow is white and crusty, melting and changing textures because of the afternoon sun. And each footstep tears away a thin layer that hides a blue, crystal-like surface beneath, a surface that's moving under our feet at the speed of six inches per year. Far below us we see no sign of our team. We figure we'll recognize a train of people roped together with Huey leading the way; we figure we can recognize Huey from a mile off.

We've been hiking over four hours when we first see it—Camp Muir. We might have seen it sooner, but it's so small and we were looking for something much larger. Like I said, there are no trees around, so the camp (nothing more than a rectangular hut made of plywood and stone) looks teeny. Oh, but things are buzzing at Camp Muir. People (*Where did they all come from?*) are walking about, filling water bottles, lining up for the toilets, checking gear and packs (but not *our* team), and sometimes just standing around and staring at the summit. The summit. There it is.

A svelte, tanned young Swedish man standing next to me, waiting for his buddies to come down, points the summit out to me. "Der eat eese!" he says. (There it is.)

"That's it?" I'm incredulous. "Nothing behind it?" I ask, remembering a thing such as false summits. "So we're looking at the summit right there? Do you see where I'm pointing? You're telling me *that's* the summit? The top?"

"*Ja!*" (Yes.)

Chera and I can only stare. It seems so close. Seems like we could just scoot right on up there. But someone tells us it's about a six-hour hike from right here. That's slow scooting. "What do you think, Chera? Same time next year? Think we can make it?"

"We can make it right now!"

She's not suggesting we go, only that we're ready. I agree. We hang out for a few moments longer. Adjusting boot straps, sitting and resting our legs. We'll boot ski back down, we decide. *Glissade,* Caroline had called it. But for now we're at Camp Muir, 10,188 feet up. Only four thousand feet from the summit. We've hiked four and a half miles, gained about forty-seven hundred feet of elevation in the last five hours. After a good half hour of soaking in the view of the summit, we figure it's time to go back to Paradise.

Plus, it'll be more impressive to be heading down when we meet up with our team.

We say good-bye to the plywood hut, offer it our safekeeping upon our return next year, and begin our descent. It's fast, easy, and fun. In no time at all Camp Muir is teeny again.

Glissading is not quite like skiing. We don't go as fast, and we constantly stop, but only long enough to push off again. And if we get a good push and the boots are turned right and the snow is slick and packed beneath us, we can slide for a hundred feet or more before we stop. *Wheeeeeeee!*

The sky is clear, gorgeous, cloudless. We're skiing into the blue, into the faces of Mount Adams, Mount Hood, and Mount St. Helens. I've never seen a sky so blue. As blue as...a swimming pool. As blue as...billiard chalk. As blue as...our underwear! We're like blue twins flashing down the mountainside. We're creating enough draft to blow our hair back, to seep around our glasses and make our eyes water, to make us drool.

Holy, holy, holy.

Holy, holy, holy.

Then we spot them! There they are! Our team! Adam skis over to us and shakes our hands. "You guys going up to Camp Muir?" he asks.

"Been there," Chera says, beaming from behind her shades.

"You're coming down?" Adam is incredulous. "You guys did great! You're higher than anything else around here." He waves a hand at all the other peaks we see, that we've already met.

"We'll be back next year," I tell him.

"I hope so."

Then I hear the voice. High and nasal. He's calling our name. It's Huey: "Hey, Pierce!"

I look up the grade a bit to where the team has stopped to rest in single file. Huey is up front. He's waving a water bottle at us. "Congratulations!" he yells. "You did great!"

Suddenly, he doesn't seem like such a bad guy at all. We beat them to base camp and got to say hello on our way down. Part of me wants to say, *Nah, nah, na-nah, nah.* And the other part of me wants to give Huey a big hug—like they do in the movies when everyone pulls together, to huddle through the storm, to avoid certain disaster. I settle on a giant wave. Chera does too. We're all three waving and teetering on The Mountain.

"See you next year!" Chera yells.

"You better!"

We say good-bye to Adam and ski away. When we stop, not far down the mountain, we celebrate. "Yes!"

"Yes!"

"We did it!"

"We beat everyone to Camp Muir!"

"Ha ha!"

"Ha ha!"

Then we sort of dance there on the mountainside: jumping, kicking out with our plastic boots, swinging our ski poles like giant drumsticks and putting all of our eyes at risk.

It takes us over an hour to come off the snowfield and reach the rock trail. As we're hiking, Chera makes an observation. "So we come here for a mountaintop experience. It turns into a valley experience, but then that turns into a mountaintop experience."

She's not looking for any sort of answer, just making an observation.

I think about this too. Yesterday she was crushed, so disappointed she could hardly eat her ice-cream cone. Now she's the happiest kid alive—and we made it only halfway up! *Do you always have to go to the top?* I wonder. We stretched ourselves today. We didn't make it to the top. We only made it to the place where everyone else was filling up their water bottles and using the toilet, yet we danced on the mountainside.

But I guess the important thing is that we reached a point no one thought we could—not Adam, not Caroline, and certainly not Huey. We believed in ourselves. Sounds trite, I know. But we stood there, six hours away from the summit, believing we could do it if given the chance, believing we could baby step it to the top. I thank God for Chera—for her heart and her grit. Chera thanks God for that angel. We talk about him on the way down. We're convinced God's been keeping a close eye on us during this trip.

Next year is our chance. Next year we'll be back. That's what we think as we descend into the valley, into a cloud that has suddenly boiled up and covers all of Paradise below. We descend down this mountain, letting the wind whip and burn our faces, knowing that next year we'll be right back here—and beyond. Next year we'll be on this very mountaintop, dancing with our plastic boots and ski poles.

We'll have to warn those around us.

7

Preparing for the Big Dance

Chera cools down at the end
of our first marathon.

W inter comes to Tennessee. We get some snow, not much, but enough to remind us of the mountain in the far corner of the country, where some of the snow we tramped on still lies, only now it's probably frozen hard beneath at least a couple of feet of new stuff.

Chera is in an all-school play, a comedy called *Dearly Departed,* playing the part of an old, old woman. Just watching her shuffle along all bent over, and hearing her talking like she wants someone in the next town to hear her, tells me she's been paying attention when we go to Grandma's house. It's strange to see her made up gray and withered, fast-forwarded through life. But I realize that's where we're all heading, that is, if we survive life's curveballs. The difference in the end will be the things that fill our heads.

This winter we train harder than ever. We run and lift weights and eat lots of meat. And as the winter gives way to spring, we run the marathon again. We want to test ourselves and to prove to ourselves that we're getting stronger, I guess. We want to break five hours.

On race day Chera is nervous. I am too until we learn there's been a mix-up with our bib numbers and someone at the start line tells us we're in corral number four—not nine (out of a possible ten). "Hey, we got a real shot at winning this thing now," I tell Chera, and she laughs.

This year it's sunny and hot before the race ever begins. No one is wearing a sweatshirt like last year. Again, because there are so many people, we can barely hear the national anthem or the distant *pop* that we take to be the starting gun. People begin to move right after that, and we jump out to a good, fast pace and feel great. We decided before the race not to take any potty breaks this year, because that had cost us a good thirty minutes last year, so we drink less and run past people waiting in line at portable potties, and urinating against the side of McDonald's, and urinating against trees and between cars like dogs and cats.

We're doing great, running in a zone. We are stronger. But then at mile eight I feel a twinge in my right knee. *(Ow! That hurts!)* I keep going, trying not to alarm Chera, believing I can run through this. It's just a temporary pain. But I guess I'm not hiding things too well because at mile ten Chera asks if I'm all right. "Just fine," I lie, and begin to swing my leg—like Frankenstein's monster—rather than bend it at the knee. At mile twelve I have to tell her I'm hurting. We cross the halfway timer at two hours, thirteen minutes, way ahead of our two-and-a-half-hour goal. I get someone to wrap my knee in an elastic wrap, and then we begin to walk—because of me. And walk. And walk. I can't run. I can't even bend my knee to make a running motion. Every time I try, especially on the downhill slopes, the pain shoots up to my hip, up my ribs, and out the top of my head like a lightning bolt. I don't know why Chera doesn't laugh. I know I look funny limping and flopping. But instead of laughing, her face darkens with concern, and she reaches out—to steady me. "It's okay to just walk," she says. And so we just walk and walk our marathon. Up the hills, then down the hills and into the valleys.

Again and again I try to run, but I just can't. But when we get to mile twenty-four I figure I'm going for it—pain or no pain. I can do anything for a couple of miles—just thirty minutes, even if I go super slow. But when I try, such a stabbing pain shoots up my right leg that I have to grab hold of my thigh and scream. I apologize. "I'm sorry, Chera. But I can't do this."

I've never done that before—apologize to one of my children for not being able to do something. Oh, I've told them, "I'm sorry, but you can't go to the mall," or, "I'm sorry, but I don't have any more quarters for that video game." But I've never had to apologize for not being able to do something important. I'm disappointed in me, and I believe Chera must be too.

Some days, after my dad had slept off all the alcohol from the night before, he would tell me he was sorry. *"Sorry for keeping you awake. Sorry for not staying sober. Sorry for not being able to stop drinking. Sorry I sold all our fishing poles, but I needed the money."* Right up till the day he died he told me he was sorry, and oftentimes he would weep. But no matter how sorry he told me he was, I'd get angry with him—angry that he couldn't stop drinking and angry that he was sorry that he couldn't stop drinking. (I could care less about the fishing poles.)

"Why don't you go on ahead and cross the finish line," I tell her, trying to sound as casual as if I'd just asked her to save me a seat at the food court. There are still a couple of miles to go. She still has a chance to break last year's finish time of five and a half hours.

But instead of running away, she grins and shakes her head and says,

"You didn't leave me on Mount Rainer, so I'll stay with you here." I know I can't compare wrestling alcoholism to running with a bum knee, but I can look at Chera's reaction to my shortcomings and only marvel. I guess I expected her to be angry.

The knee's not so bad that I have to lean on Chera, although that would be a touching scene to cross the finish line like that. But I do hobble like one of those grandpa characters from the play she was in earlier in the year (and the gray in my hair is real). In her spirit Chera carries me those last two miles. We cross the finish line at six hours, ten minutes. We've just walked the entire last thirteen-point-one miles. As poorly as we finish, there are still people limping, gimping, and flopping across the finish line behind us as we make our way to the car.

Oh, they'll all get their medals, I think, *just like we have, but did any of them learn about mercy—or grace—like I have from Chera?* What may have seemed such a small thing to another man, I see as the unquestioned, unearnable love it truly is.

And I'm released to accept my failure—by her love.

Summertime. On the day Chera calls home from sea level, from San Pedro, Belize, I'm building a bridge—a real one. She's seventeen now and on a mission trip with a group from camp, with Larry and Lori. She calls to say she's helping to clean up one of the worst alleyways for drug dealers in the world. ("Don't talk to strangers!") And that they're witnessing and telling people about God. ("Okay, but make sure they're nice strangers.")

In the meantime, I'm in a valley, up to my ankles in mud, raising up pressure-treated lumber and marking it so I can haul it back out of the mud and cut it with a handsaw. We have a small farm out in the woods and a small lake in the very bottom of a deep valley. It's shaped like a pear, plump on one end and tapered to nothing at the other. At this small end, a tiny stream feeds into the lake from the peaks above. So when it rains, all the runoff is carried down this carved valley and into the lake. I decided to build a bridge over this small valley so anyone wanting to hike around the lake could do so without getting wet or muddy—plus it'll look quaint.

So while Chera's raking up trash and glass from a sandy, drug-infested alleyway, I'm driving nails into wood, thinking that one day someone will walk around this lake, come to a stop on this very bridge, and gaze over the water. Perhaps he'll pray. Perhaps she'll talk out problems with her spouse. Perhaps he'll propose—all right here on this bridge. That's why everything has to be level and straight. I don't want a man going to one knee on my bridge and tipping over.

It's all about reaching people, I think, *with a rake, with a hammer and nails.* We have to touch people, treat them nice, tell them about God, give them a bridge to cross over the muddy valley. I pull free from the sucking mud to go get more nails. I feel good about this simple action: each nail I drive brings me one step closer to building that bridge.

Still two months before we go back to Mount Rainier. Chera is back from Belize and working at camp. I decide it's time to step up training. I find a new trail not far from home. There are some big hills on this trail, and it's about two miles round trip, so I begin by running it, slowly at first. After a few days of running, it's time to strap on the backpack and get used to that. I have to find something heavy to put in the pack, so I look around in the garage and find, there in the corner, some heavy boxes. I know they're heavy because I've already moved them half a dozen times, from one side of the garage to the other. There are six boxes and all are filled with two-dollar-off coupons for a Chonda tape—my wife's new comedy video. Since they're nearly expired, I stuff every pocket I have with them. The pack gets heavy fast, and I make a mental note to give Chonda credit as trainer. Now, everywhere I go, she'll always be right there behind me.

Late summer. Chera's back from camp and we're running and packing every day, and I push us both like one of my old high-school football coaches used to do—the same one who made me take salt tablets when I was near dehydration. I don't know that much about conditioning, but still I tell Chera, "Come on, push it! Run through the hurt! Just a bit more! Last hill and then we're home free!" (I say that one a lot.) I even sound just like my old coach, except that I leave out, "Here. Take a salt tablet and keep going!"

We're going to be ready this time.

> Be ready in the morning, and then come up on Mount Sinai. Pre-
> sent yourself to me there on top of the mountain. (Exodus 34:2)

As we hike, with our packs filled with books, magazines, Chonda coupons, and clunky shoes (that was the heaviest thing Chera could find in her room), we talk. Chera tells me about her new boyfriend—Tom. (Patrick has moved away.) "He says I might be the one he marries," she tells me.

Ow! That hurts!

"But I've still got five years of school before I even think about marrying," she adds.

That's right!

"Why do you think he said that?"

I search for the right words. They must be good words, I realize. Perfect words. I must wax eloquent. I must espouse absolute truths. I come up with, "To keep you from"—my voice is starting to rise; if that happens, then this sentence is in danger of becoming a question, which will undermine my authority on this subject, so I keep my voice steady, and at the last second decide to add a quick "probably" to the end—"breaking up with him, probably." Was that perfect? I don't think so.

She adjusts her pack and sighs and says, "That's the way they are, I guess."

They. She means boys. I used to be one of the *theys*! Shoot, I still am. I remember how *they* are, still know how *they* are. But now, in this situation, I'm working for the other side—the side my daughter's on. Yes, with all the vehemence and fervor of Paul, I have changed my ways. And I will do whatever is necessary to inform *(protect?)* my daughter from *they*, which is us, which is boys.

"Yeah," I say. "That's the way *they're* wired, and you just have to be on guard for that sort of stuff from *them.*"

"I'm not going to date any one person exclusively for at least a year," she tells me.

"That's probably a good idea," I say, believing it to be a really great idea.

"And if anyone wants to take me out, I'm going to tell them that they'll have to ask you first," she says. I stop to take a drink of water. I wonder if she'd been watching *Little House on the Prairie*—that episode where Laura likes this new boy in town named Frank and—

"Don't worry," she tells me, taking the water bottle from me. "I'm not going to send *everyone* your way. If I think they're too creepy, I can say no right away."

"You don't worry," I tell her. "I don't mind chatting awhile with them before I say no." She grins. I think she likes me acting as gatekeeper. We finish our walk.

The next day Chera tells me that a boy named Matt will be, *may* be, calling—if he doesn't chicken out. A few hours later I answer the phone and it's him—the boy. Chonda is there listening.

"Yes, Matt," I say. My voice is so low I'm fearful that I won't be able to maintain that register. "I appreciate your calling." *Appreciate your calling?* Who talks like that? "Chera told me you'd be calling. I appreciate this." *Again?* "I'd just like to check your plans for tonight."

"Yes sir," he answers, his voice thin and winded. "I thought we would go to the mall." He stops. That's it? No food? He's not going to feed my daughter? I didn't raise her this long just to stop feeding her because some boy who likes to walk around the mall won't stop and buy her a hamburger.

"And maybe get something to eat?" I lead him.

"Yes sir. We can get something to eat."

"So I guess you'll get back at what? Eleven?"

"Yes sir. Eleven."

"P.M."

"P.M. Yes sir. And I won't have anyone else in the car with me."

I hadn't thought of this one. "Good. Good." I say as if that were my next question. "That can be dangerous. Okay then. I'll tell her that everything sounds okay with me. Again, Matt, I appreciate your calling."

"Thank you, sir."

I hang up and Chonda's grinning at me. " 'I appreciate your calling'?" she mocks.

I shrug. "Seems like a nice young man," I say. "Says 'yes sir' a lot. Sounds like he's going to buy her a hamburger."

How long can I protect her like this? Will Chera's dating a nice young man ever feel okay? I'm thinking no.

A few hamburgers later, Matt is at the house. He and Chera are watching television—*America's Most Wanted.* I walk by and see them glued to the television screen. "Good show tonight?" I ask.

Chera looks up, but Matt keeps watching. "Matt's cousin is on tonight," she explains, almost in a library whisper. She notices my confusion and explains further: "Matt's cousin is one of those who was shot to death at the Captain D's last summer. Did you hear about that? They still don't have a clue who did it."

Matt doesn't look up, but I can hear his pain, eking out his pores—out of his hair—echoing out loud and long through the valley.

It's two weeks before we climb, and we hear a story on one of the cable news channels that there's been some activity on Mount Rainier, some rumbling, some melting and mudslides. Rocks as big as cars have tumbled into the valleys. The story reminds us that there's a volcano with unfinished business up in the northwest part of the country. We're not worried, though. Our friends think we're crazy, but we're fine with that. We know what's waiting for us up on top of that volcano.

It's a week from summit day, and I go to the outdoor-gear store and browse the aisle with my basket, willing to purchase whatever it is we're going to need for this climb. I get a new pair of gloves for Chera, a couple of water bottles (blue for me and pink for her), and some new underwear. That's about it. Of all the things made available here—sleeping bags, cooking equipment, kayak stuff—supplies stacked up like cords of wood, I buy underwear. I did the same thing last year, so I'm hoping it's a different cashier this year. I'll die if I get up to the checkout and the same kid scans my merchandise and asks, "Hey, didn't you buy some underwear about this same time last year? Yeah, now I remember. It was blue, as blue as…well, bright blue, wasn't it?" But no one recognizes me or mentions my perennial buying habit.

As I leave, I think about those Christmas afternoons so long ago, leaving my grandmother's house and hearing my own mom saying, "You can never have too much underwear." Here, today, a week before I'm supposed to summit Mount Rainier, I realize this is an absolute, inarguable truth. We *needed* underwear then; we *do need* underwear now; we'll *always need* underwear in the future. Clean underwear is basic to preparation.

This year, the color is black—the color that's made up of all colors, the color of focus, the color of determination, the color of dominance, a color that will contrast the white of the glacier even more so than the blue had. I believe I've made a wise choice and a wise purchase.

We are packed and ready to go. We couldn't be any more prepared, not only because of the undergarments, but also because we'll have support and encouragement, and someone to bring along the sausage links: Larry and Lori are going with us.

8

The Man Who Lives at the Top of the Volcano

Chera poses with the sunglasses
given to her by an "angel."

It's been thirteen months since Chera and I tried to climb Mount Rainier. She'll be eighteen in a few months. An adult, she reminds me. It's hard to believe we're back at The Mountain. Today it's raining, and the locals tell us this is normal—not like the sunny day they had a few weeks before. I think we're making Larry and Lori nervous because Chera and I reel off one mountain story after another—stuff we've read over the winter. It's *The Pierce Family Show* in a minivan.

We're in a rental car, driving up the mountain from the hotel. There's a restaurant in Paradise, and I thought it would be good to grab a bite to eat there, and maybe, just maybe, we'll get a glimpse of the mountain. We unloaded all the luggage at the hotel, except for the ski poles, so they're clinking in the back as we make slow, sweeping curves (loops, sometimes). Going up. The sun punches through fluff here and there, but so far, no mountain. And just as Larry and Lori are beginning to think we've hoodwinked them, that we made the whole thing up, we round another turn and I see it first. "There it is," I say. But everyone is looking too low. I point upward, to the top of the front window. And to see what it is I'm pointing at, they have to bend forward, head down to the dash of the car, and look up through the top of the windshield. Now they see it.

"Oh wow!"

"Oh my!"

"Oh!"

The sight takes my breath away. A familiar feeling. Cold and majestic. Wispy clouds blow past like torn cotton let loose in the wind. For no more than fifteen seconds we see the massive shape, bordered in blue and spotted with jagged, rocky outcroppings. And then, just as suddenly as it had appeared, the mountain disappears behind the clouds. We're still pressed to the windshield, eyes wide, like someone with an eyeball pressed to a camera's shutter when it blinks, and now he can't believe that's all he gets to see. We think we know where it is. We have it pinned down behind all that fluff, only it's not coming out. We drive on farther, staring at the white sky as if it were a friend's house and we were on our way home from school. Just want to know if you can come out and play? No. Not today. See you tomorrow.

We order something to eat at the Paradise Inn—things that are seared, sautéed, and marinated. Between the four of us we have cow, salmon, and buffalo. We sit there in dim lighting beneath a web work of pine logs that are almost black with the patina of time, wood smoke, and seared salmon. A fire crackles twenty feet away. If the fog were gone, we'd be able to see the mountain, but for now we have to settle for the drawing on the menu. We're trying to explain to ourselves why we're doing what it is we're about to do.

"Climbing is never the same," says Lori. "We've done the same mountain in the Appalachians dozens of times, and it's always different."

I mention how Moses went up the mountain, and how he brought something down that would help others.

Lori nods. "It's living in the valley with the perspective gained from being on top," she says.

"Yeah," I say, "like what Moses did."

"It's more than the view," says Larry.

"You can get that from an airplane," says Lori.

"How else do you explain why a blind man will climb Everest?" adds Chera.

"It changes you," I say.

Silence and reflection.

All: "Again. And again. And again."

That settles that question.

Larry's intent on hydrating himself and encourages us to do the same. The waitress is quick and on top of things, but she can hardly keep up with our water glasses. We talk more about climbing, the sights, what mittens to wear and when, blue bags (which we'll use for potty breaks), and what it'll be like in the bunkhouse at Camp Muir. I'm beginning to think seeing the mountain for that brief moment was not such a good idea. It's easy to see we're all a bit nervous. Yes, here at Paradise, there's definitely a strong commingling of salmon and dill, buffalo and garlic, fear and respect.

Then Chera, adjusting her plate so that the meaty part of her dinner is directly in front of her (and the rice-looking stuff away), says, "Well, tomorrow is a big day for me."

Tomorrow is training and evaluation. If we don't make it past tomorrow, we won't need mittens, and we won't sleep shoulder to shoulder in the bunkhouse. We'll all go home. She remembers last year. And how can we not think about it? Since we got here it's been nothing but, "Oh, remember that bench, Chera? We sat there and ate ice cream (after we failed the evaluation). Remember that pay phone on the front porch of the general store? That's where we called home from (after we failed the evaluation)." Everything is pretty much like we'd left it: beautiful, majestic, simple, ageless—

and a reminder of what didn't happen. And The Mountain is the greatest reminder. But Chera's not the same. She's stronger, so much stronger. "You are so ready," I tell her. And I believe it with all my heart. I'm glad I told her so. Maybe my being able to tell her things is one way the mountain has changed me.

Larry and Lori have never attempted anything this big. Maybe that's why they admit that they're a bit concerned about the evaluation as well—in spite of the forty-mile bike trips they'd made every day for the last month as a part of training.

It's going to be a long night. I'm ready to go back to the hotel and watch the Weather Channel.

Back in the room Chera and I repack our bags super light. We work quietly but efficiently. We adjust crampons, discuss the merits and the downside of fleece and Gore-Tex, and how we'll benefit or suffer from either tomorrow. We fit our lamps to our helmets and tie our ice axes to our packs so they'll pack safely until we need them. *Where did we learn all this stuff? Mountain climbing stuff?* I wonder. A lot of it we learned last year—the year we failed the evaluation. So even our knowledge is a painful reminder.

Since we go to bed early, I wake up at 4:00 a.m. and have to make myself sleep until 6:00. As I'm sitting up and pulling things together, I remind Chera that it's already 8:00 at home. She doesn't care. Her body's already on Seattle time, so she sleeps longer.

I go to the lobby and find the complimentary bagels. Shortly, Larry and Lori join me. We're wearing our plastic boots, and they squeak so much when we walk that we can hardly hear. The bagels are good, so I eat two of them.

We try to be casual, carefree, talk of weather, wildflowers, and Mount St. Helens. (There are posters of it—pre-eruption and post-eruption—all over the lobby.) Okay, it's time to leave, and why are we making this so scary?

The Man Who Lives at the Top of the Volcano   175

"Is everybody here?" asks our guide and instructor for the day. I wonder how the people who aren't here are supposed to speak up for themselves. "In just a moment we'll take a brisk walk up to the snowfield—and I do mean *brisk*. Now let me remind you this is an evaluation, and it's strictly pass/fail." He makes minimal eye contact. Even he seems to hate this part. We're disappointed we didn't draw Huey this year.

The weather is beautiful for today's test. The sky has cleared, and the mountain has come out to play. We take time to lace and relace boot strings and apply and reapply sunscreen. We even smear a bit of the SPF 40 around the rims of our nostrils. "Sun reflects off the snow," Chera reminds us. More useful mountain knowledge.

When the signal is given (the guide yelling out, "Okay, let's go for a walk!"), we hoist our packs—so light from what we're used to, without all the Chonda coupons, that we feel we must be cheating. Larry falls in behind the guide. Lori follows Larry so she can match his pace, like they've practiced. I drop in behind Lori, and Chera follows me, to match my pace. Of the thirty people in the school that day, we're the first four behind the guide for our brisk walk. *What are we doing?*

"We're doing it!" I hear Chera say.

The first part of the trail is paved, and thirty hikers in plastic, squeaky boots sound remarkably like a train leaving the station. Other people, families with small children and tourists taking pictures, move over and let us pass. They stare at us, at our gear. Some think we're crazy, we can tell. Others seem to admire us, want to salute us.

An older Asian man and his wife are walking along slowly, his hands buried in his jacket pockets. We seem to surprise them. He backs to the side and covers his wife with a protective arm. He makes eye contact with me and asks, while pointing to the top of Mount Rainier, "You go to top?"

He glances to the top of the mountain; he looks back at me. I smile—big, happy, genuine. "Yes sir," I say, never slowing down. It's the same answer I've been giving for the last year.

He drops his hand and buries it back in his jacket. He seems shocked by my answer and says with a heavy accent, stressing every syllable, "Im-pos-si-ble!" *Funny how he chose that word,* I think. I'm reminded of a list of adjectives for mountain climbers from an old book called *Golden Age of Tension Climbing. Impossible* is one of those adjectives: *"This adjective, along with inaccessible, is long gone into limbo; the nineteenth-century writer used it to describe climbs subsequently made by girls in their teens. And no one will repeat his mistake."* The man shakes his head and says, "It take you all day?"

By then I'm too far ahead to answer, but I hear Chera sing out, *"Two days!"* I glance back and see Chera grinning. The old man is shaking his head again.

Even though we're moving so briskly, everything is strangely familiar: the trails; the endless steps made of cedar and pine logs and square stones; the wildflowers, lavender and red; scrubby bushes and gnarled trees; red rock; green ridges below us that look like ripples made on a calm, green lake; the switchbacks; all so familiar and—oh yes!—there's Mount Adams, Mount St. Helens, and, if I squint, I see the conical head of Mount Hood from Oregon in the middle. We're back! And we're moving up one switchback after another—*briskly.* The air is thin and cool this time, unlike the draining heat of last year. Our packs are lighter. We're pressure breathing without being told. Every time I look back at Chera, she's grinning.

But Lori's having trouble pressure breathing. Shoot, she's having trouble just *breathing.* She has asthma. She steps to the side of the trail. "You guys go around," she says. "I just need a minute."

We're at the steepest of the switchbacks now. A long series of up, up, up. Our guide slows the pace. Hallelujah! When we turn, we see Lori. She's not far behind and has fallen in with the second half of our group, keeping pace there. She waves and we know she's all right.

No matter how fast our guide walks, he can't shake us. And even though Chera falls three times, she never drops out or loses her place.

Thud.

I look back. Chera is on all fours, scrambling to her feet.

"Are you all right?" I ask.

The man behind her retrieves her water bottle and stuffs it in her side pouch. ("Thank you.")

"My bootlaces," she says, as way of explanation.

We brisk walk through the same series of switchbacks where things went wrong for us last year. We're up much higher now. Things are less green and more gray, and there's red rock and—

Thud.

I look back, and again Chera is scrambling—but it's a brisk scramble.

"Are you okay?"

The man behind her again retrieves the water bottle and tucks it into her backpack. ("Thank you.")

"Bootlaces," she says.

Now we can see the snowfield where we'll train. Again, it's all strangely familiar—déjà vu familiar. "Dad, we're doing it!" I hear Chera say. From here to the snowfield the trail is rolling and rough, but the steepest part and the switchbacks are behind us. From here on in—

Thud.

I look back just as Chera pops up. She's blushing. She thanks the man behind her for once again helping with the water bottle.

"I'm going to fix this bootlace when we stop," she says.

We've come two miles, gained over a thousand feet of elevation, and we're not even breathing hard. We stop on an outcropping of large, smooth boulders and remove our packs.

"Let's rest and eat a bit," our guide says.

Chera looks at me, smiling way too big for snacks. "We did it, Dad! We did it!"

I give her a big hug, and Larry takes our picture. We've worked a year for this moment. To everyone else it was only a brisk walk up some steep trails, but to Chera and me, it's been the greatest victory so far. We split a pack of gummy bears.

One of the first maneuvers we practice on the snowfield is the self-arrest with the ice ax: drop to a knee, drive the pick end of the ax into the ice with a shoulder behind it, kick in some buckets (little footholds) with the toes of your boots, and hold it. We do this together, the whole team, and since we're suppose to look away from the ax head, I'm poised there on the ice, staring out at Mount St. Helens and the blue, blue sky—holding my position until the instructor can come by and assess what I've done (either saved my team or killed my team). I'm holding it right there, three points in the snow—two feet, one shoulder. My cheek melts a spot on the ice. I can't see him, but I can hear the instructor behind me as he checks the others: "Yes. Now this looks good, *real* good," he says. "And that's a nice aggressive kick too. I like that. What's your name?"

"Chera Pierce."

"Great job, Chera."

From my awkward position there on the ground, and from my front-row seat of the volcano across the way, not even a re-eruption of Mount St. Helens could have thrilled me more.

We spend the rest of the day practicing with the ax, with rope, with stepping and sliding. At the end of the day, we hike down and our guide gives us final instructions about the climb tomorrow. We passed. Looks like we're going up. We're so excited when we leave that we hike across the parking lot and into the hotel lobby with our backpacks on and celebrate by buying some ice cream.

Chera calls home and tells her mom all the important parts. I catch some of it:

"The only girl in the first group!… Perfect technique with the ice ax!… Aggressive!"

Wow! What a big day. The only thing bigger will be to climb the mountain. And we'll start that tomorrow morning.

Im-pos-si-ble!

Oh, he shouldn't have said that.

Our packs are ready. We've checked and rechecked them more than once. The sky is gray this morning and spitting just enough rain that I have to turn on the wipers from time to time. It's 8 a.m. and we're driving to the trailhead. We're not talking much, and when the clouds blow past for a second and we can see the mountain, Chera sighs softly, "That's a big mountain." No one else says anything for the rest of the way.

We're the first ones at the guide house, so we do a quick equipment check with one of the guides:

"Ice ax?"

"Check."

"Crampons?"

"Check."

"Sunscreen?"

"Check."

We're ready, and so we wait for the rest of the climbers—twenty-four today. And there'll be six guides going with us. We break up into two groups of twelve, and our group follows a guide named Ben out the door and to the trailhead. He's tall and wiry (of course), and we stand there for a moment as he gives us the last bit of instruction. "How do you eat an elephant?" he asks. I'd never thought about that. "One bite at a time," he answers himself. And then, without any fanfare or friends or family cheering us on, or even curious onlookers who might want to admire us or possibly envy us, we begin our ascent of The Mountain by following Ben, who's still wrestling an arm into his backpack as he says, "Okay, let's get it."

We start at fifty-four hundred feet. The fog is soupy and makes droplets of water on my fleece sleeves. Chera walks behind me. I glance back and say the obvious: "We're climbing Mount Rainier." She grins back.

Fog covers the scenery and seems to be tugged back on a need-to-see basis, like the way one of my teachers from long ago would cover the questions to a quiz on an overhead projector and reveal them one at a time. We see red and purple flowers along the trail's edge, but no farther. We walk past a deer, so close that I can reach out and touch her with my ski poles. But mostly I can only see the trail, so I watch the boots in front of me—totally focused. I think the boots belong to Larry.

We hike up for an hour before we take our first break. Water puddles on the glasses that hang from a string around my neck. The wind blows stronger, and Ben advises us to put on our hooded rain jackets. This helps keep the wind out of my ears, but also blocks everything to the right and left, narrowing my field of vision even more. *Just watch the boots.*

We hike for another hour and make it to the snowfield where we take another break. Here Ben suggests we put on our crampons, to keep from slipping. And since we're now on the snowfield, we sit on our packs in the spitting snow and rain and apply more SPF 40 sunscreen to our ears and noses and cheeks and the backs of our necks. It's colder now and the sunscreen is like paste. I dump the water from my glacier glasses and put them on, and this helps with the invisible UV rays that bounce off the snow. But when they fog up, I can only see what looks like the heel of a boot in front of me (Larry's?). I just follow that.

Our group of twelve pushes on up, dressed in hooded jackets and glacier glasses, leaning into the mountain, pushing with our legs and ski poles against gravity and the blustering wind. There are times when the wind stops for several steps. That's when I can hear the ice crunch beneath my boots, beneath the twelve steel spikes that puncture a nice and neat pattern every time. If I take the time to connect the puncture marks, I believe, I could draw a cabin in the woods, with a nice little fire crackling in the fireplace...

My mind wanders all over the mountain, but somehow I manage to put one boot in front of the other. Chera is right behind, in step. All I can see of her is her mouth. It's open and she's breathing hard.

Right in the middle of the snowfield I can see a giant rock pile, and it looks as if we're heading for it. I can't see them, but I can hear the moment when the first of our group reaches the rocks. Their crampons click like marbles dropped on a tile floor—sporadic, without rhythm. When I reach the rocks, I learn why. The stones we have to walk across are all different sizes. I find I make the most noise when I step on the big rocks, but they're also the most slippery, and every time I slide it sounds like six fingernails skating across a chalkboard. *Screeeech!* My backbone tingles. So I try stepping on the smaller stones. But they wobble, and suddenly I'm surfing and punching madly right and left with my ski poles for some sort of purchase. So then I try the smallest stones, the pebbles. But they're loose, and my feet sink and shift and slip, and every step takes a tremendous amount of energy. Twelve of us *click* and *screech, click* and *screech* across this giant, expansive rock pile. So slowly.

When we get to the ice again, Ben says, "Great job. Now let's go." I thought we'd been going! No break yet? My legs are getting tired, and Chera is slowing down. But no break yet. Only more climbing. We're high up on the snowfield now, when suddenly we punch through the clouds and into the sunlight and blue sky. My glasses clear and I can see below us a sea of white, billowy fluff. So beautiful to look at, but I know from experience it's really cold and wet. Chera's in front of me now, and I'm saying things like, "That's good, Chera. Keep going. Breathe. Blow out those candles." The slower hikers step aside. We pass Lori, and I encourage *her* to blow out the candles. She looks at me like I'm crazy—or maybe she's just tired. Shortly after that, Chera steps aside and tells me to go around. She's terribly fatigued—or maybe she's just tired of hearing me talk about candles.

I trudge on and glance back from time to time to make sure she's moving. Slow and steady, but she's okay. My eyeballs find Larry's boots and I latch on. *One step at a time,* I tell myself (as if I would think to take any more).

If anything, as we climb higher, the wind is worse—stronger. I can't feel my toes, fingers, or face anymore. I see boots. I see ice. I see something fall from my face. What was that? I see it again and realize it's leaking from my nose. A thick, clear syrup. I can't sniff fast enough or strong enough. Besides, sniffing takes too much energy. So I concentrate on taking steps (one at a time) and ignore my nose and what's happening there.

Then my legs begin to sing. Not a song I recognize, just general singing. My calves are pounding out low notes, and my upper legs are screaming like a girl. Together they're making some sort of jangled music. I glance up—boots. I glance back—Chera's still moving. No one else seems to hear the song coming from my legs. I trudge on.

By now I want to go home. I want to quit. I'm sorry I came, and I don't know why I came. I can't remember anything that's happened before. I don't know why I'm here. I don't know where I came from. I don't even remember my name. All I know is that something's coming out of my nose, there's an awful opera coming from my legs, and I'm supposed to be taking one step at a time—

That is, until we come to a crevasse—a big split in the ice that has no bottom, or if it does, it's filled with helmets, water bottles, and all sorts of other hiking gear, maybe even hikers, so says our guide. Here I have to take an extra wide step to cross. I do and my legs crescendo; my nose explodes. But this horror only lasts seconds, then I forget everything that just happened, and I trudge on, going up, one step at a time.

We can see Camp Muir. That's where we're going. Up ahead, against a backdrop of red, craggy rocks is a rectangular, flat-roofed, squat building with four windows facing us. We saw this last year. My memory slowly returns, and I recall hearing that inside are bunks, with soft pads to lie on. I suddenly remember I have a daughter and that there was a crevasse a while back—several of them. I get to the edge of the snowfield, to the loose rock that leads up to the only flat spot I've seen in almost five miles, and look back.

There she is. Trudging along, leaning into the mountain, blowing out candles, and listening to the song her legs are playing. I throw my arms up in the air, as if she'd just scored a touchdown. She sees me and wipes her nose with the back of her hand. One step after another she comes. She makes it to the camp, and since it's impossible to hug with all this gear on, I give her a loving shake and say something positive. We undo our packs and lay them next to a rock wall and then pile other big rocks on top of them so they don't blow away—even though they weigh about thirty pounds each.

We stand there for a moment, side by side, almost five hours since we'd left the guide house, looking back down the mountain. The wind that blows up and into our faces keeps us from tipping over. The ice below us, a cracked mirror, shoots straight down and looks way too scary to walk on (like we just did). This expansive ice field disappears into the clouds below, but it's easy to tell where the ice ends and the clouds begin because the ice looks hard, black, brown, and red from the stuff that washes over these higher rocks and paints this side of the mountain. The clouds are simply white and fluffy. Way out in the white fluffy stuff, we see the snowy peak of Mount Adams.

The moment here at ten thousand feet is poetic, or should be. "Let's get inside, out of this wind," I say. Nothing poetic about that.

"I'm going to the latrine first," says Chera.

"I'll save you a bunk."

Camp Muir is named after famed Sierra Club founder John Muir. There are several pieces to this campsite. Some stone houses—two, I think, made from stone quarried right there. (Why haul stone up ten thousand feet when it's all around for the taking?) There's a row of latrines, made from wood, with real toilet seats. But since they're compost toilets, when you open the lid you can see (and smell) Mother Nature doing her decomposing chore right there before you. There's a helicopter pad (obviously a much later addition than the John Muir years). This is where supplies are carried in, like propane used to melt the snow to make water and then to heat the water so that we can mix our instant dinners. And there's a bunkhouse. This is the squat, rectangular building I saw earlier. It's built of plywood and two-by-fours and two-by-sixes, all cut unsquare and uneven. Or perhaps they were cut square and just nailed together crooked. Or perhaps it's a beautiful piece of carpentry, but the wind has wracked the whole edifice, creating so many unparallel and uneven lines inside. But it's windproof, and because of this, it's a sanctuary. My mind suddenly races back.

It was hardly a sanctuary, this dull gray, cinder-block building, but Dad wanted me to pray with him. He begged it of me. So I knelt down and did my best.

I'd moved away to college and left Dad all alone, and could only visit once a week. With no one there to pour out his beer, or help him to bed, or drive him to wherever he needed to go, I was sure he was going to be in serious trouble. But Dad had friends in our small town; the mayor was one of them. He allowed Dad to live in the concession stand there in the park, now that it was winter and there was no baseball.

It was the same park where I'd played baseball as a kid. The unpainted building was small and rectangular, and the only window, used to serve refreshments through, was large, but it was now boarded over with plywood and crooked two-by-sixes. Inside, the bulky, square stainless-steel machines—like a hot-dog cooker and popcorn maker that smelled of burned grease and butter and mouse feces—hibernated for the winter and were just as cold. On one counter was a row of spigots promising Dr Pepper, Coca-Cola, and Sprite with just a touch of a button. Underneath this was a spaghetti tangle of plastic hoses that were sticky to the touch. If you sat still long enough, pretty soon you'd see a mouse silently run the loop of a hose. And if you got real bored sitting there staring at the hose, hoping to see a mouse, you could always chuck something at the creature when he did show up.

Dad's cot was at one end of the building, next to an extra-deep, stainless-steel double sink. There was one chair there in the room, one the mayor had brought from his house. It was big and broken in and so comfortable that sometimes Dad would sleep in it. I knelt by him there in the gray, squat building, feeling defeated by the familiar smell of stale alcohol that he breathed my way when he said, "Please pray for me."

I did. But the prayer was a grueling uphill climb. I wasn't sure it was going anywhere.

There's barely enough room to move about inside the bunkhouse once everyone shows up. Three rows of bunks, wide enough that six people can lie there shoulder to shoulder, line one wall. That's eighteen sleepers. Six more can lie in the high bunks over the door. That makes twenty-four. We toss our bags to the top bunk and climb up the ladder. (The ladder is so nicely crafted that I figure it must have been built back in the lowland and helicoptered up.) It's only five in the afternoon, and we're changing socks, hanging up wet fleece, and eating junk food. (My gummy bears are frozen and harder to chew.)

Ben comes in with red nose and cheeks and gives us a talk about what to expect tomorrow.

"Go ahead and eat, get comfortable," he says. "Drink plenty of water, so much that you have to go to the latrine at least once in the night. If you brought earplugs, now is the time to use them. Let's see"—he looks at his wristwatch—"it is now…6:00. At 6:30, let's all be horizontal and trying to sleep. You're going to need it. We'll be in sometime tonight to wake you, and then we'll head to the upper mountain."

"What time?" someone asks.

Ben shrugs. The other guides shrug. "Some time between 11:00 tonight and 3:00 in the morning," he says. "Depends on the weather. Any other questions?"

Silence.

"Good night, then."

I'm lying on the top, against the windowless wall. Chera is lying beside me, and next to her is Lori, then Larry, then a woman from Kentucky and a man from Germany. It's still bright outside, so I lie there staring at the ceiling, at the patches in the plywood over my head. There are twelve of them in the four-foot-by-eight-foot sheet above me. There are nine in the one next to it. Some big, yellow, rubber-coated hooks jut out from the ceiling and walls. Hats and harnesses and headlamps hang from these, like bats from a cave ceiling, draping low, touching sleeping bags. If I turn my head to the right, I can see out of one of the small windows. From here it could be a frame holding a masterful painting of Mount Adams. I'm tired, but I can't sleep. I look at Chera, but I don't see her because she's buried herself in her bag.

I count the patches in the plywood again—twelve. The one next to it—nine. I can't sleep. The room slowly dims because the sun is setting. I can see its final glow for the day reflecting off Mount Adams. No one's talking now, but there's still too much noise to sleep. Someone's eating potato chips—chips and not cheese puffs. I hear Velcro fasteners ripping apart, the hissing of polypro against polypro (slick against slick), sniffing, hissing, zipping and unzipping, a cough. Did someone just scratch? And then there's the wind. Roaring, growling, snarling wind. It rushes around the mountain and then slams into our squatty building, splitting apart when it hits the sharp, (un)square corner and passes along both sides. I place my hand against the wall and feel its vibrations. I wonder if twelve patches in the plywood over my head are too many.

The wind roars like rain pounding on tin. Then suddenly, as if on cue, it ceases and the world is silent—except for the hissing, sniffing, zipping, and unzipping. The (un)silence is only momentary. The roar returns like an ocean wave against rocks.

Someone opens the door. I sit up and see going out that person (man? woman?) in a helmet and a headlamp. Bathroom break. I'm reminded to drink more water, and I do.

I have no watch, so I don't know how long I've been lying here, listening. People slip out, trying to be silent, but with big clunky boots and headlamps and wooden bunks and a door that swings freely, it's impossible. Lori goes out three times, Larry once, then Chera takes a turn. I drink more water. My turn's coming.

How will they wake us? I wonder. *Flashing lights? Blaring horns? What time will it be?* We'll have to use our headlamps. It'll be cold outside, where the backpacks are. We'll have to fasten our crampons in the cold. Make the loops with the long straps, work the tricky fastener while we're tired and cold. I wonder what time it is. I'm starting to float, to rise from the pad, like I usually do when I fall asleep. My arms and legs are gone. I'm so light. Rising to the patched-up, plywood ceiling—

I have to go to the bathroom.

I sit up and dig around for my helmet with the headlamp. I won't turn it on until I'm outside. And I'm not even going to try the boots. Not now, not from the top bunk. Like a tall coal miner in a short shaft, I make my way along the top bunk in a duckwalk, down to the ladder, tiptoeing over the feet of Chera, Lori and Larry, the woman from Kentucky, and the man from Germany. I find the ladder with my hands and back down in the dark, praying I'm right about the craftsmanship of this ladder.

I make it to the floor, where I step on something with Velcro on it and drag it to the door before I can kick it loose. At first the wind doesn't feel so cold. Sort of warm. Not bad. I step onto the ground. The crushed rocks don't hurt, but the bigger, sharper ones make me dance. *Ow! Ow!* I can't go back for the boots now. One hundred feet to the latrine. I can go a hundred feet. I'm halfway there when I stop. I brace myself by bending my knees. My back is to the wind, arms out as if I might push it back. I'm wearing a large fleece sweater. But I believe if it were an extra-large the wind would pick me up and blow me off as if I were a kite.

I see light below. Must be Seattle. The moon is hanging there high up, unaffected by the wind. It's bright and round and lights up the glacier below, full of craters and cracks—the glacier, that is. Mount Adams is a photographic negative. Where there are ridges and valleys and peaks, I see only lines. And, although I know I can't, I feel as though I can see the whole world from atop this volcano.

The wind subsides for its momentary rest, and I hobble quickly to the latrine.

Back in the bunkhouse I climb the ladder, step too high, and bang my head. I'm grateful for the helmet. Slowly I duckwalk to my corner, remove the helmet, and settle into my sleeping bag. I hear the wind splitting in two and rushing around the cabin, then silence, then sniffing, then hissing. The roar returns in seconds. Only this time it begins to work as a lullaby. I'm about to fly away, about to slip on the extra-large fleece and sail off the mountain, when I hear a soft, friendly voice call out:

"Rise and shine, everybody. Time to get up."

So that's how they do it, I think. Instead of loud, clanging cymbals, they wake us with a soft, singsong greeting. At least he didn't say, "Let's get it." I sit straight up and see one of the guides below, circling the room, his beam of light a saber swishing the darkness with every move of his head. "Rise and shine," he sings.

Chera comes out of her cocoon and I hear her say, "It's 1:00 a.m."

I haven't slept at all. And now it's time to go to the upper mountain.

In less than a minute, the buzzing of activity in the cabin is almost louder than the roar of the wind outside. Lights come to life here and there, upper bunks and lower bunks. Zipping, unzipping, hissing, mumbling, more zipping and unzipping, jangling of harness belts, clicking of helmets on floor and ceiling. The clunking of plastic boots on wooden floor and ladders. Twenty-something hikers come out of their sleep (or near sleep) and try to ready themselves for an early morning climb up a glaciated mountain.

The guides bring in hot water, and the cabin is soon filled with the aroma of chocolate, coffee, and oatmeal. Chera moves quietly and deliberately, wrestling into her boots. "I can't believe we're doing this," she says. "Are you nervous?" she asks me.

"A little," I say, my voice too high because of the altitude, and I'm thirsty and we're in the top bunk. I can't make the snap work on my helmet. "We'll do all we can and see how far we get," I tell her.

"All right," she says. "Then let's do this." She ties her bootlaces on the first try.

We're outside in fifteen minutes, stuffing our water bottles into our packs, keeping a knee on anything we don't want to blow away, like an ice ax or crampons. It's just like I'd imagined earlier from my cozy corner bunk—cold and miserable. Headlamps are throwing light about haphazardly, hitting backpacks, bootlaces, and people's eyes.

Guides are calling names ("Brown! Dillon! Hardy!") and instructions ("Make sure your harness is tight! You should be wearing your parkas! Stay warm! Crampons tight, everybody! Hook into your rope team now!"). Chera and I are on a team with two people we don't know. The plan is to travel harnessed in single file, with fifteen feet of rope between us. And instead of ski poles, now we carry our ice axes—in the perfect grip that many learned only yesterday.

Larry and Lori are in a group ahead of us. They take off, and five minutes later we head out, lamps on, even though the glacier glows like a moon. Ahead of us, and moving up, we see two trains slowly snaking up the glacier. We make up the third.

I'm behind the guide and Chera is behind me. The two people we don't know are at the end. Before we begin, our guide instructs us to pack away our parkas so we don't overheat. So we pull them off and, despite the blustering wind, stuff them into our backpacks. We set out with a slow pace, one bite at a time. *This is not too bad. We can do this,* I think. We're on Cowlitz Glacier, climbing steadily and slowly. Mostly I watch the rope in front of me, allowing it to drag along in the ice, but not so much that I step on it. (I know that much.)

Sometimes I feel the cord draw taut behind me, and Chera's effort, push, and struggle are communicated back through the cord like a telegraph.

If anything, the wind is worse on the exposed glacier. Sometimes it blows us from behind and we get a free step. But mostly it pushes us from the side, trying to drive us into the ice. We walk across a snow bridge that spans a crevasse that my light won't fill. *Hurry, Chera, and make it across before the bridge can cave in.* I think this thought through the cord. She makes it, and so do the two people at the end, whom we don't know.

Now we're walking along a ridge so narrow I can't put one boot beside the other. Above us are loose rock and ice that sometimes tumble down. Below us is sheer, slick ice for a thousand feet or more. We move quickly along this ridge because our guide says it's a falling-rock zone, and we don't want to dawdle there.

We traverse a crooked route across Cowlitz Glacier, maybe three-quarters of a mile, when we come to a high, rocky wall that appears too steep to climb. But I see points of light making crooked lines up there and know that's where we have to go.

We coil up our ropes and carry them up the rock. Each step is uncertain because of the looseness of the rock, the weakness of the legs. Again there are big rocks and little rocks, and every step is filled with sound *(screech)* and uncertainty. The ridge is at least two hundred feet up. At the top is Cathedral Gap. A nice, respectable name. Halfway there, Chera collapses.

"Are you okay, Chera?" the guide asks.

I help her to her feet. She reworks the coiled rope in her hand. "I think

I'm done," she says. The effort to be heard above the wind takes more energy away.

I've been ready to celebrate since we got to Camp Muir. My legs are gone. From the bunkhouse to here has all been extra, a bonus. *Let's go home. Let's dance in celebration right here and now because we've come this far. Let's go back to the little squatty building on the flat spot.*

"Let's get to the first rest stop and you can turn around there," says the guide.

More climbing?

But Chera doesn't protest, so neither do I. She nods, and her lamp blinks a yes. And so we keep climbing. Sometimes the wind gusts so greatly that we drop to all fours and hold on to the mountain until it passes. Sometimes tiny stones, pumice, I learn, and pieces of ice whip up into our faces and blast us with hundreds of tiny, sharp points.

Chera wants to sit down, I can tell. No, she wants to lie down, to curl up in a fetal position and rest. I know I do. But she pushes herself higher and harder. We're getting closer to the top of this ridge, though that's hard to believe. Prayer is working. The guide swaps Chera and me around on the rope. This way he can tug on her rope, move her along. I'm shouting encouragement into the wind, and so are the two people behind us.

Then, as impossible as a periwinkle taking root at the base of a glacier, Chera pulls herself up to the crest of Cathedral Gap. She seems taller, wiry. The rest of us make it up, and our group stands there a moment. From this vantage point it's easy to see where we've come from and where we're going. We see behind us the glacier we've crossed and know that Camp Muir is there in the dark somewhere. And before us lies an expanse of white, all fluffy and pure, like a cotton courtyard, leading up to the old, unchanging face of Mount Rainier. *A tall, wiry man could scoot right up its chin, along the bridge of its nose, and sit upon its head,* I think. We're standing in the doorway of the mountain's cathedral.

We see a circle of lights just ahead of us on the glacier. That's where we're going. Our guide takes off. He tugs on Chera's rope, and she slips away from me and trudges farther up the mountain. In a couple of seconds, I feel a tug on my rope and follow after her, pulling along the two people we don't know.

We follow the lights, and when we get closer, we see people we recognize sitting on their packs, and there's Larry and Lori. Chera drops her backpack, drives her ice ax into the ice, and announces through her ragged breathing, "This is *my* summit!" I know what she means. It's over.

We dig out our parkas and move fast to zip in the heat we've generated. Then we sit on our packs and wait for instructions about how to climb down, to go home. Seven of us are going down in this group. Lori goes back with us, but Larry stays and heads out with a few others. We watch him walk away until he's nothing more than a point of light in a chain of lights that snake over the rocky steps that make up the mountain's chin, close enough to touch its face if he wants to.

My father's skin was so weathered and deep with lines, that for the longest time I had imagined his face to be as hard as stone. I allowed my palm to follow the side of his face and rest on his cheek. I patted it in a parental way. "Dad, are you going to wake up?"

I was just out of college and would marry Chonda in another month. Since I had my own apartment, Dad had moved out of the concession stand and in with me. It was an efficiency with the bed, television, kitchen sink, and fish aquarium all within an arm's reach. To make the most of our space, we bought a set of bunk beds.

As hard as I tried, I could never completely cut off Dad's flow of alcohol. While I was gone, or else late at night, there would come a tapping on our ground-floor window. Dad would answer, and quickly and silently beer and money would exchange hands. I hated him for this.

Because of the lung cancer he'd battled for the last couple of years, Dad didn't get out very much. Every night I'd climb up to my bunk and try to sleep in the haze of cigarette smoke that would pool there near the ceiling like a cloud, while Dad would sit in a kitchen chair and talk—mumble mostly. It was usually dark, and all I could see was the fiery orange of the burning tobacco every time he'd inhale a tainted breath.

I left one morning and came back early afternoon, and Dad was still sleeping. He usually watched game shows at this time, so right away I knew something was wrong. His breathing was labored and ragged. "Dad?" I called again. No answer. "Dad, are you okay?" Still no answer. Now I sat on the side of his bed and placed a hand on his shoulder and gave him just a slight jostle. "Dad?" A sinking feeling passed over me. He'd fought the alcohol and the cancer for the past two years, but now the fight was over. He was enjoying his rest.

Yet still I tried more jostling, and I spoke louder and repeatedly. Finally, I shifted around until I was fully into the bottom bunk and lifted his head and rested it in my lap. His forehead was warm and soft, not made of stone at all. So I began to stroke his face—forehead, cheek, the bridge of his nose. Every inch, I touched. At first I thought he was crying, but the tears were mine. I told him I loved him, again, and again, and again.

Then a most miraculous thing happened to me. For the first time since I was a child, I believed I had found God: he was there in the warmth of my father's face; he was in the unconditional love I had withheld for so long, but finally expressed at that very moment. "I love you," I said for the hundredth time, and held him for as long as I could. A wall had collapsed, and behind it stood God with his arms open. There, on the bottom bunk in a tiny apartment, I had reached my summit.

Almost a year later, Chera was born.

Someone tells us we're at eleven thousand feet, at a place called Ingraham Flats. Chera and I sit on the floor of the white sanctuary. She leans against me, trying to rest, trying to stay warm. I put my arm about her shoulders and hold her there. It's about 4 a.m. The moon is still out, and from here we can see the world. Then I realize where we are. We're on his front porch—the man who lives at the top of the volcano. This is where he sits and watches and smiles and cries because of us. Here is where he makes wind and snow and sunshine. Here is where he kicks back, with his feet resting on Little Tahoma Peak on the other side of the valley. Here is where he welcomes his guests and offers them a seat, and when he really wants to entertain you, he hangs a full moon up above so you can see his handiwork.

Chera is buried inside her parka. I give her a tight squeeze. She's so tiny that I'm amazed how she was able to push herself to get this far. But then I realize this is where she's been heading for a long, long time. There was no stopping her. Her will and her desire had lifted her like a breeze lifts a kite. "We're up here, Chera," I tell her, happy to announce the news. She lifts her head wearily, and all I can see of her face are two dark and tired eyes, deep in the padding of the parka. "We're up here with the man who lives at the top of the volcano," I say.

She's smiling. I can see it in her eyes. She remembers the television show.

"I always pictured it warmer than this," she says.

We sit on our backpacks on the glacier and we wait, beneath Orion's belt and a glowing moon, looking out over the valley. Soon we'll be going down. We're not at the very top, but we don't have to be. Like Chera said, this is *our* summit. We battled wind, ice, rock, gravity, and cold. God sent angels to push us on, to hold us up, to encourage us, and to give us sunglasses when we needed them. And then, when we were totally spent and exhausted and could move no more, he gave us a resting place on his front porch. We can hardly move. But in our hearts we are thrilled. So, there, deep inside our parkas, we rise with arms lifted up, and begin to dance.

Descending

I walk beside Chera, about to give her away.

After three years and five mountains and many valleys, this story must now end, although our journey will continue—after all, I am her father. In case you're wondering, Larry made it up to thirteen thousand nine hundred feet before the guides spun the small group around because of the weather and safety concerns, only five hundred feet from the top. No one made it to the summit that day.

I guess there are a lot of reasons for climbing a mountain—like fresh air, scenery, and exercise. Chera and I talked about reasons a lot, usually while we walked over hard trails, or ran for mile after mile, or at dinner before a big climb, or over ice cream at the mountain's summit or base, or while we read over maps and travel brochures. Somewhere in all that talking we discussed that question: *Why?* And what we came up with is that we don't climb mountains simply because "they're there." That's too simple. And we don't climb them for the view. Like Lori said, we could see that from a commercial jet. We climb mountains because of what we bring down—mainly an experience with *what* we are made of: strength, perseverance, determination, and honesty. To recognize these attributes in yourself is glorious; to make use of any one of them is incredible; to see them plainly and clearly in your daughter is overwhelming.

But can't you discover these attributes in other ways? In less grueling ways? Perhaps. But where else can you see your daughter wrap the blistered heels of strangers with the last of her Band-Aids? Or hear her exclaim, as you climb to fourteen thousand feet, "How can people say there is no God?" Or watch her as she sits on the ice and straps on a pair of crampons, with a cold wind blowing at thirty miles an hour, and the whole time she's grinning?

And just what did we learn from all this mountain climbing stuff? We learned about perspective. Lori says the hill at her house will never look so steep anymore. Larry says that God is big, and we are small (important, but small).

We learned where to live life. Chera taught me that it's not always about making it to the summit—it's about *going.* The summit is small, usually, and you're only there for a moment. But the journey… We visit the summits, but we live in the valleys. That's where we train. That's where we prepare. That's where we grow strong. For that lesson, I want to tell Chera "thank you." But that's like saying Mount Rainier is a big mountain. You can't come close to conveying the size of it in words.

I heard a story not long ago: George Leigh Mallory and his climbing partner Andrew Irving did not return from their attempt of Mount Everest. It was Mallory's third attempt and Irving's first. Saddened and crushed, some members of the failed team returned to Europe. A few months later one member was giving a lecture about what the team had learned of the mountain in spite of the tragedy. In the middle of his lecture, he interrupted himself and turned to a large photograph of the mountain affixed to the wall behind him. He pointed to the image of the mountain, his face reddened with anger and something like a personal hostility. "You!" he said to the photograph. "You, Mount Everest! You have turned us back once, and a second time, and even a third time. But one day we will defeat you. Because you can grow no taller, but *we can grow stronger!*"

You have the ability to grow bigger and stronger. You work, you train, you focus. You run when you're tired. You pack when you're aching. Then one day you're ready. You shower and shave and brush your teeth. You buy some new water bottles and some black underwear (or blue). You fly to the right state, take the rental car to the trailhead. You skip the sandwich this time, and you begin to ascend for a different reason now—the promise of ice cream no longer a necessary enticement. You push into the wind and the snow, pulling yourself and your nose, coated in SPF 40 sunscreen, up the ice. You climb all night—even though you want to rest—and by daybreak you summit. You stand at the very top—or somewhere pretty close—with nothing higher for a thousand miles. The sun rises and wants to know what you're doing up here, so high up, so dangerous. Below, the birds shake their heads and call you crazy. You hope someone is down there, perhaps by that lake that's glimmering cobalt blue and looks no larger than a thimble (although you know it is). You hope that someone is taking a photograph that will wind up on a calendar or a place mat in a restaurant, or on a coffee mug or key chain. Then, there you'll be, all over the country (and especially in the Seattle area) hanging on walls, lying on dinner tables, hanging from a trucker's belt loop, so tiny and insignificant that not even the world's most powerful microscope can prove that you really are standing there. But you are. And you will stand there in complete and utter awe because you've never seen anything so expansive. The only things that even come remotely close to describing the sight are those three dots at the end of a sentence that indicate that, even though the sentence must end because of paper and ink and those sorts of constraints, the idea behind the sentence just keeps going and going...

Then, just when you feel like you are absolutely the highest thing on earth, God looks down and says, "Oh, there you are. I knew you would make it. Would you care to dance?" That's when you throw your head back and raise your arms upward as if stretching, and your feet will begin to move. That's what it's like at the end of a climb. Those are the kinds of things Chera and I brought down with us. And those things have changed us.

After lots of searching and weighing and visiting, Chera finally decided upon the college she wanted to attend. From the pick of any university in the country, any place in the country, she decided upon one about twelve hours away from home, in Tulsa.

She can't see it from her dorm room window, but if she steps outside and turns a corner, she's got a great view of a tower that, when the sun is just right, appears to be setting behind the peak of a mountain. To this day, every day, someone carries a bundle of prayer requests to the top to pray over them. From all over the world, people—old people, lonely people, hurting people, little boys standing on linoleum kitchen floors—still write down their prayers to God and mail them there.

Chera and I visited the campus a few months before school started. It was the first time I'd been there since I was eighteen. Everything seemed much smaller (like it always does when we look back), except for the tower. We walked around it and passed through its shadow, and eventually we rode the elevator to the top together and walked the windowed circle, awash in light. In the center of the tower, away from the windows, I noticed a closed door with a sign that read Prayer Room. While Chera looked out over the golden campus, I reached out and placed a trembling hand on the door. Slowly I traced my fingers over the raised letters. *Here is where* my *climb started long, long ago,* I thought. In the room on the other side of this door, in the form of a simple letter, is where I called out to God.

In the time it took to take a couple of breaths, I imagined someone passing through this door with a bag full of letters, all with three-cent stamps stuck in one corner, and emptying its contents onto a big table. I imagined seeing my letter slide off a tall pile and a loving hand gently scoop it back to the center, where it was bathed in prayer. God can move mountains, that's true. But sometimes he just moves people up mountains—neither is easy, and both are miracles.

I had been wrong, I thought. God *is* here indeed, at Chera's new home.

I passed on by the door before I would cry. I never told Chera about my earlier climb, and I certainly didn't tell her about the Prayer Tower, but I imagine she'll read this book, and then she'll know.

What I do now, because I know I have to, is unhitch the rope that binds father and daughter together on this mountainside. As I type these last remaining words, I squeeze the carabiner to the thickness of a rope and let the cord drop slack between us, careful not to step on it with my crampons. After that, she will move, walk, and climb to areas far away from me, far above me, completely untethered, forced to call on all the skills she's learned on the way up. But she can do this. She is able. I know—because I have seen her in the valley, and I have seen her on the mountain.

Epilogue:
Six Years Later

Chera and I pose on the most
important day of her life.

It's an easy enough task to do, considering what we've done over the years: scrambling over boulders, kicking buckets into the side of a glacier for a better foothold, lugging fifty pounds of backpack up six thousand feet of elevation gain. Over the past six years, we've climbed five more mountains and run four more marathons and half marathons. So this should be easy. The short walk from my back door to the flat spot down by the river is only about a hundred feet. And there's a brick path with smooth, level steps. All downhill. Could hardly be called a climb.

Chera and I stand at the top of this slope and gauge the lay of the land like you do when you're about to take a hike. To the right are some big boulders bordered by rhododendrons. Near the bottom and by the small river sits a four-piece string quartet. The music has no problem climbing the slope to us. To the left, nearly a hundred and fifty chairs fan out into the shaded, deep green grass, all filled with people wearing their finest, who now stand and smile at us. Chera's arm is hooked into mine. I feel her squeeze, and she asks, "Are you ready for this?"

It's the same question she asked so many years ago as we set out to conquer Mount Rainier. But this is bigger. Much bigger. So I try to think of something to say that will rightly capture this moment. "This is a big day," I whisper back, and then wonder if I could possibly make any greater understatement.

Our destination, our summit today, is unlike any other we've set out for in the past. Waiting for us at the bottom is a young man named Craig. A year earlier he and Chera drove to the top of Tiger Hill, where Chera and I had run and trained for weeks on end. There, next to a double-wide trailer and some barking dogs, he proposed. He said he chose that spot because he believed it meant the most to her. And she said he was right.

Today my job is to simply climb down this small slope with her on my arm. To stand next to her and her husband-to-be and wait for my instructions. Unbeknownst to me, everyone in our soon-to-be-combined families has bet on which step I will break down and lose it. Many have chosen the first two because they believe I will be overwhelmed with the sight of family, the stirring music, and the overall gravity of this day. I come close at step one. My lip quivers once. But that smooth, level step number two has a wobble in it that Chonda has reminded me a hundred times to take care of. As long as you know it wobbles, there's no problem. So I had spent most of the time at rehearsal cautioning people to beware of that wobbly second step. But even though you know it's coming, the teeter back and forth will still catch you off guard.

The step wobbles, we teeter, and Chera says some mountain-climbing thing. It's something technical, something I'd heard her and others say dozens of times out there on the mountain—so familiar that I immediately forget what it is she said. But the simplicity of it is so comforting that I laugh instead. And she does too. We smile and chat all the way down—not too much unlike we had done hiking down Pikes Peak (only without the singing). And no bets are won today—not on my tears.

I stand between Chera and Craig. She still has an arm looped in mine. My brother-in-law Michael is performing the ceremony. He waxes eloquent about why we are all here and what this day means in the lives of Chera and Craig as well as everyone else there. I can hardly stay focused because I know what's coming. At rehearsal, this is the point where I lost it. In the ceremony Michael doesn't sound out my instructions, only nods. But in my head I recall what he said the evening before, while all were casually walking through their roles, occasionally laughing. And as he nods I hear those words that had rolled over me like an avalanche: "Now, David, you take her hand and pass it over to Craig and let go."

Let go? Just like that?

Yes, just like that. So on this day, with her dressed like royalty and me in a tuxedo, I clasp the tiny hand that squeezes my arm, lift it, and pass it over the space of a couple of feet. And when I place her tiny fingers into Craig's waiting hand, he clasps her hand with the certainty of a carabiner. I think I even hear the *click*. And that's how I'm able to let go and turn and walk away so I can sit next to her mother.

I try to pay attention to the rest of the ceremony, but I guess that's what pictures are for and where that video guy we hired will come in handy. Instead I think about the note that Chera gave to me the night before— along with the gift: a Snickers bar framed in a shadowbox that now hangs on my office wall. The note says, *I just want you to know that this is not the last of our adventures together—just one more peak to add to our list. Besides, I finally found someone who can keep up with us!*

And that's what it's all about—not just climbing and running—but having someone to share that with. So many mountains ahead of them. So many miles to be covered by foot. I should cry—even tears of joy—but the part that wants to laugh takes over, and I work to suppress it.

Not until later, as the dance floor clears and Chera and I dance to "Christopher Robin," do I cry, and so does she. I used to sing that to her and play it on the guitar when she was just a little princess...

So as we dance, I remove a handkerchief (hardly used) from my tuxedo jacket and pass it to her...

It's a long song, and the band plays every verse. So we do what we've always done at the top of every mountain: we dance.

Discussion Questions

1. Why does David decide to take Chera up on her suggestion to climb a mountain? Do you relate to his sense of time slipping away? How have you responded?

2. How did you feel about David's decision to join his daughter in climbing Pikes Peak?

3. Have you ever wanted to do something that seemed unusual or out of character for you? What happened? Is there something you've wanted to do that you might try with your child or spouse—maybe skydiving, snowboarding, pottery, or travel?

4. Does David's thought at twelve thousand feet on Barr Trail about the short trees with strong roots relate to you and your child's relationship either previously or currently? How do you think you will need to redirect your energy during the next few months as you weather the coming changes in your relationship?

5. Have you discovered similarities between parenting and searching for God? In what ways have you experienced or imagined parenting to reveal God or vice versa?

6. Chera and David's first attempt to climb Mount Rainier ends in failure. But within a few hours, what seems devastating becomes an incredibly fun memory. Have you had times that go from terrible to great? Can you see how God was at work?

7. Chera and David had some real valley moments. Think about how the journey through the valleys helped them make it to the summit, and how time at the summit helped them make it through the valleys. Can you point to a time in your life where this was the case with you?

8. After Chera and David's first climb of Pikes Peak, Chera was ready for another adventure, but David was wrestling with a fatherly adventure: advising his daughter about dating. After reading about their first climb, can you compare the unique challenges of that to fathering? Just for fun, which would you prefer?

9. After Pikes Peak, David seems to get serious about training. He joins a gym. But when he and Chera decide to run in a marathon, he once again underestimates the value of training and preparedness. Can you see a real parallel with parenting and preparedness in general? How do things change—on both fronts—as the story progresses?

10. As David leaves Chera with her group at Mount Audubon, he struggles with telling her good-bye and how he really feels—that he's proud of her. Why do you think it's hard for David to be honest at that moment? Can you see his childhood experiences influencing this moment?

11. After the first failed attempt at Mount Rainier, David is quickly protective of Chera. How have you handled your child's disappointments in the past? Did you buy her ice cream? Was it difficult to allow your child to be disappointed? Describe some moments where you see David and Chera growing together as a team after this.

12. During the second marathon David says he experienced grace and mercy from Chera. Compare that to some of the childhood stories he's shared up to that point. What do you think he was trying to say?

13. Compare Chera and David's second climb of Mount Rainier with the first one. How were they stronger that second time—physically and emotionally? How did your thinking about the "man who lives at the top of the volcano" change from the beginning of this book to the end?

14. What sort of lessons did Chera and David bring down from the mountain? And how did they manifest themselves (for example: discipline, determination, self-esteem)?

15. What do you think about the man who gave Chera the sunglasses? Was he an angel? Could he have been an angel? Share your angel story.

16. Even at Chera and David's second trip to Mount Rainier, they are overwhelmed at the majesty of this mountain. Have you had moments where God's creation leaves you awestruck? How did that affect your relationships with those who shared that experience with you?

17. At Chera's wedding and at every summit, what do you think the significance of the dance is?

Acknowledgments

I want to thank Larry and Lori Nellist, who introduced us to the great outdoors and continue to do so; Dr. Ayne Cantrell, who referred to me as a writer long before I ever did; Bill Jensen, my agent, who believed in me from day one and promised to take me to his secret steelhead fishing spot since day two; Mick Silva, my editor, and especially his two daughters; hang on to them—like fathers do; my son Zachary, whom I'm writing about next, as he continues to teach me how to be alive; Mike Courtney, who was with me when I got the call, who has always told me I was going to get the call; Doris Courtney, for taking care of my wife all those years out there on the road; Michelle Mitchell and Victoria Fister, for keeping me professional; Alison Evans, for keeping me sane, and Ken Evans, for believing I'm famous—and telling everyone so; WaterBrook Multnomah, for your commitment to plumb the wellsprings of faith; Chera, for pushing me and keeping me from growing up too fast; and Craig Meredith, for loving Chera the way you do.

DAVID W. PIERCE has published many short stories in *Alfred Hitchcock's Mystery Magazine* and *Ellery Queen's Mystery Magazine*. An adjunct English professor at Middle Tennessee State University and an avid fly fisherman, he lives with his wife, Chonda, and his son, Zachary, in Murfreesboro, Tennessee. You can learn more about David at www.davidwpierce.com, and you can learn more about his daughter, Chera, at www.squaresheep.com.